10 THINGS I ~~HATE~~ LOVE ABOUT MONEY

10 THINGS I ~~HATE~~ LOVE ABOUT MONEY

SIMPLE RULES TO SPEND AND SAVE YOUR WAY TO WEALTH AND HAPPINESS

BY

MAT MEGENS

WILEY

This edition first published 2025
© 2025 John Wiley & Sons, Ltd.

All rights reserved, including rights for text and data mining and training of artificial intelligence technologies or similar technologies. No part of this publication may be reproduced, stored in a retrieval system, or transmitted, in any form or by any means, electronic, mechanical, photocopying, recording or otherwise, except as permitted by law. Advice on how to obtain permission to reuse material from this title is available at http://www.wiley.com/go/permissions.

The right of Mat Megens to be identified as the author of this work has been asserted in accordance with law.

Registered Offices
John Wiley & Sons, Inc., 111 River Street, Hoboken, NJ 07030, USA
John Wiley & Sons Ltd, New Era House, 8 Oldlands Way, Bognor Regis, West Sussex, PO22 9NQ, UK

For details of our global editorial offices, customer services, and more information about Wiley products visit us at www.wiley.com.

The manufacturer's authorized representative according to the EU General Product Safety Regulation is Wiley-VCH GmbH, Boschstr. 12, 69469 Weinheim, Germany, e-mail: Product_Safety@wiley.com.

Wiley also publishes its books in a variety of electronic formats and by print-on-demand. Some content that appears in standard print versions of this book may not be available in other formats.

Trademarks: Wiley and the Wiley logo are trademarks or registered trademarks of John Wiley & Sons, Inc. and/or its affiliates in the United States and other countries and may not be used without written permission. All other trademarks are the property of their respective owners. John Wiley & Sons, Inc. is not associated with any product or vendor mentioned in this book.

Limit of Liability/Disclaimer of Warranty
While the publisher and authors have used their best efforts in preparing this work, they make no representations or warranties with respect to the accuracy or completeness of the contents of this work and specifically disclaim all warranties, including without limitation any implied warranties of merchantability or fitness for a particular purpose. No warranty may be created or extended by sales representatives, written sales materials or promotional statements for this work. This work is sold with the understanding that the publisher is not engaged in rendering professional services. The advice and strategies contained herein may not be suitable for your situation. You should consult with a specialist where appropriate. The fact that an organization, website, or product is referred to in this work as a citation and/or potential source of further information does not mean that the publisher and authors endorse the information or services the organization, website, or product may provide or recommendations it may make. Further, readers should be aware that websites listed in this work may have changed or disappeared between when this work was written and when it is read. Neither the publisher nor authors shall be liable for any loss of profit or any other commercial damages, including but not limited to special, incidental, consequential, or other damages.

Library of Congress Cataloging-in-Publication Data is Available:

ISBN 9781394299751 (Paperback)
ISBN 9781394299768 (ePub)
ISBN 9781394299775 (ePDF)

Cover Design: Wiley
Cover Image: © Hammad Khan/Getty Images

Set in 11/16 pts and Minion Pro by Straive, Chennai, India

SKY10105135_050725

This book is dedicated to my mom, dad (RIP) and my four kids: Molly, Michael, Marilyn and Makenna. My mom and dad inspired my vision for HyperJar in equal measure with their lessons on spending money carefully and avoiding the perils of debt. I still remember my mom saying to me that more people need to know how good it feels to save up for something. Truer words have never been spoken.

My children's unconditional love and support has been a constant positive force in my life and inspires me to achieve everything I have. Kids, I hope you all read this book and remember its lessons well.[1]

> 'If you know the enemy and know yourself, you need not fear the result of a hundred battles. If you know yourself but not the enemy, for every victory gained you will also suffer a defeat. If you know neither the enemy nor yourself, you will succumb in every battle.'
>
> —*Sun Tzu,* The Art of War

> 'If you're trying to sell it to me for full price, you've picked the wrong girl.'
>
> —*Elle Woods,* Legally Blonde *(Robert Luketic, dir., MGM, 2001)*

---

[1] If not for yourself, for me in my retirement.

CONTENTS

PREFACE ix

FOREWORD xi

INTRODUCTION xiii

SECTION I
WHAT 1

CHAPTER 1
    RULE 1: FOCUS ON YOUR DAILY SPENDING 3

CHAPTER 2
    RULE 2: UNDERSTAND YOURSELF 19

CHAPTER 3
    RULE 3: UNDERSTAND OTHERS 41

CHAPTER 4
    RULE 4: THE SMALL THINGS MATTER 61

CHAPTER 5
    RULE 5: MASTER DEBT. THE GOOD, THE BAD AND THE UGLY 79

CONTENTS

SECTION II
HOW — 103

CHAPTER 6
RULE 6: AUDIT YOUR SPENDING HISTORY — 105

CHAPTER 7
RULE 7: BUILD NEW HABITS THAT WORK FOR YOU — 127

CHAPTER 8
RULE 8: SPEND LESS BY FINDING DEALS — 151

CHAPTER 9
RULE 9: ENJOY THE JOURNEY (AND BUILD A SUNNY-DAY FUND) — 179

CHAPTER 10
RULE 10: BEGIN SAVING AND INVESTING DAILY — 201

CHAPTER 11
BONUS RULE 11: PARENT GUIDE FOR HELPING YOUR KIDS — 231

CONCLUSION — 247

ACKNOWLEDGEMENTS — 249

ABOUT THE AUTHOR — 251

INDEX — 253

PREFACE

If you asked most people who know me to sum me up in a few words I think you would get pretty much the same three main responses: Canadian; finance guy; really into sport and fitness.[1]

Why on earth is this in any way relevant for a book about money?

I grew up in a modest middle-class family on a farm in Canada with a strict father born in the Netherlands during the Great Depression. My dad was frightfully scared of debt and was extremely sensible with money. The only debt he ever had was a mortgage on the farm which was paid off within a decade. Subsequently both of my parents were extremely focused on financial education for me and my siblings, never missing an opportunity to regale us with terrifying stories of the evils of borrowing and materialism, and the wonders of savings and financial prudence.

A nerd through and through, I started my career as an electrical engineer during the dotcom boom, working in various crazy start-ups, which gave me a lifelong love of entrepreneurship, and perhaps an unhealthy tolerance for risk.

I eventually earned an MBA and leveraged this into jobs at two prominent investment banks in London.[2] I worked in various highly technical roles in trading and structured finance in the bond markets. Many of the crazy complex financial products I specialised in were right at the

---

[1] I did test this out, there were some other words, especially from my ex-wife, but this is a book about finance so moving swiftly on.
[2] Lehman Brothers and Morgan Stanley. Not all banks are the same, despite what I imply in this book.

PREFACE

epicentre of the Global Financial Crisis in 2007, which, to say it provided an entertaining learning experience is a gross understatement. I continued to work in the financial sector for the next decade as I started a family with all the responsibility, both financial and personal, which that entails.

Throughout my journey sport has always been a huge part of my life, I am a qualified personal trainer, I play ice hockey, cycle, run, workout[3] as does everyone in my family. Exercise is so fully integrated into every aspect of our life that I barely have to think about it at all, it just happens.

You would think that: given my education and upbringing; my ability with numbers; my long career in finance (both from an intellectual angle and also having been fortunate enough to be handsomely paid at various great jobs); my personal responsibility to my family; and my disciplined approach to physical fitness; that my level of financial fitness would have been equally as high. You would be wrong.

For most of my adult life I have had a terrible relationship with money, both in terms of management, but also in terms of all the anxieties and worries that not getting a grip on finances can bring. I finally sat down in my early forties[4] and had a long hard think about why this was, and I think I worked it out.

The first result of this epiphany is that I have finally reached a place where I am genuinely happy in terms of my relationship with money.

Secondly, I founded a company called HyperJar, a visual spending app to help people spend their money better. HyperJar currently has almost three quarters of a million users, has won many awards, and is one of the most highly rated personal finance apps in the United Kingdom.[5]

Thirdly, I have written this book. I hope you enjoy it.

HyperJar is making a difference, and I hope this book helps to continue this very personal mission of mine.

---

[3] In fact, you name a sport, I am almost certainly into it.
[4] I am now 50. Go me.
[5] Permit me to be a little bit proud. The next big release in 2025 is going to be even better. We have learned a lot.

FOREWORD

For two of the three (or so) decades I have been working in finance, your fearless author Mat has been a friend of mine and, on three separate occasions, a professional colleague. Firstly, in a big American investment bank where we mucked about with all sorts of esoteric financial nonsense. Secondly, as a partner in an asset management firm (which I founded), where we boldly attempted to set the world of international trade finance to rights – well, we did right up to the time when Mat made the (frankly financially ludicrous) decision to abandon me to embark on a "career" as an entrepreneur. As you are about to find out when you read the book, Mat can put forward ideas in uniquely compelling ways, so seven years ago he managed to convince me to team up with him for a third time, at his start-up fintech called HyperJar. Many of the ideas in this gem of a book have evolved from talking to our (now over) half a million customers in the United Kingdom about how they do (or more usually do not) get a grip on their financial health – it has been and continues to be an eye-opening journey.

What I hate about the book is how Mat has used me, several times, as a prime example of what people do wrong when managing their financial (and physical) health! (I can see myself in the pages, and I hate the fact that he is completely right – I really did have to have a long hard look at myself as soon as I put the book down.) I'm going to warn you, you are probably going to have a similar reaction, but sometimes looking in the mirror is just the medicine you need to provide motivation for change.

What I love about the book is how simply and clearly the core principles are set out. I flipped between facepalming at all the obvious stuff (which I simply hadn't thought properly about, so maybe not as obvious as I thought); laughing out loud as various institutions and commonly held ideas are rightly speared; and being intrigued by some genuinely new and fresh ideas about how to look at money – particular stand-outs for me are the Daily One Number for managing your day-to-day spending and Mat's Spending Personality Index for working out if you are just a regular, or a total, nightmare when it comes to managing your money.

I hope you have as much fun and get as much out of reading this book as I did. I believe the pages contain a small number of clear foundational principles about getting to grips with money which, if put into practice, can make a genuine difference to financial well-being with real knock-on effects to overall happiness. The most important part is how simple and manageable the principles are.

I'm really interested to know what you think.

Spend life well.

Paul Rolles

INTRODUCTION

This book does not contain a magic formula for wealth. I'm sorry.[1]

What it does contain is a very simple set of rules and principles for how to understand and manage the messy reality of money. This book builds a foundation of habits that will make everyone, even wealthy people, happier with their lives.

On first glance, it seems very obvious why having money, or the lack of it, is important. We use money to buy things that we need, or in order to buy things that we want. But dig a little bit deeper and it becomes clear that there is much more to it than that:

- How financially successful we perceive ourselves to be can often be a major driver of self-esteem, either directly, or in terms of how we think others view us and our place in the world.
- How much money we have squirrelled away for the future to cover retirement or unexpected problems, has a major impact on how we feel about life today.[2]

---

[1] For both you and for me. There simply isn't one. If there was, I would own an ice hockey franchise and a great deal more cars and motorbikes and probably wouldn't have got around to writing this book.
[2] Even if the money is never needed. The quote 'you can't take it with you' may be true, but it can certainly encourage bad behaviour. Simply having a nice financial cushion for the future can make a big difference to your happiness now.

INTRODUCTION

- Feeling uncomfortable with understanding the complexity of finance and money can be overwhelming and stressful – and it can be a continuous form of low-level torture that never goes away.
- Worrying about other people, family and loved ones, and if they will have enough now and in the future, can extend your levels of stress from personal to your social networks, creating a multiplier effect.
- Being in debt, for many people a semi-permanent state, can be one of the most stressful aspects of modern life.
- There are plenty of people, with plenty of money, who still have plenty of issues and anxieties surrounding their finances.

To put it simply, money worries can have a massive impact on mental health, no matter who you are, or what your actual financial situation is. Some (not remotely fun) facts about the United Kingdom for context:

- 39% of UK adults don't feel confident managing their money.[3]
- 34% of UK adults reported feeling anxious about their financial situation in the past month and 10% feel hopeless about their financial situation.[4]
- 46% of people in problem debt also have mental health problems.[5]

So, the statistics on mental health problems and money are pretty stark. I can't imagine that this is much of a surprise to anyone reading this, but the magnitude of the problem is quite something isn't it? I'm not a

---

[3] Source: Financial Conduct Authority (2023) *Financial Lives 2022 Survey*, July, https://www.fca.org.uk/financial-lives/financial-lives-2022-survey, no author.
[4] Source: Fundraising Regulator (2024) *The Public's Experience and Expectations of Charitable Fundraising*, Opinium Research, https://www.fundraisingregulator.org.uk/sites/default/files/2024-05/The%20public%27s%20experience%20and%20expectations%20of%20charitable%20fundraising%20%2029%20May%202024_.pdf.
[5] Source: H. James and A. Lymer (2023) *Money and Pension Service: Money and Mental Health Rapid Evidence Review*, March, https://www.aston.ac.uk/sites/default/files/2024-08/final_maps_money_and_mental_health_rea_july.pdf.

Introduction

betting person[6] but if I was, I would gamble a few quid on pretty much any person, even those who wouldn't ever consider themselves having any mental health issues, having a low-level constant stream of anxiety relating to their money.[7]

What is it about money that seems to always bring with it big dollops of stress? I think I may finally know the answer to this question in so far as it relates to myself, and hopefully this book is here to try and see if these rules can help you.

I'm going to pause for a second and draw an analogy with physical health and fitness here.[8] There are thousands of books on health, diet, fitness and how to live to 100.[9] There are endless fads and experts, the next new thing in terms of working out or dieting and entire TV channels dedicated to selling you fancy new gadgets, but, when it all comes down to it, they can all be boiled down to about four principles which will get you 90% of the way there:

- Eat decent food, and eat fewer calories than you burn.
- Get some exercise – some walking, some stretching and some weights will do.
- Get enough sleep and try not to be too stressed.
- Don't do incredibly stupid things which will kill you, like smoking (at all) or drinking (way too much).

That's it. I've just saved you hundreds of hours of time and thousands of hours of worry. Just do the four things above and don't delay.[10]

On first blush, finance seems even more complex and overwhelming. Not only are there just as many crazy books, fads and people with advice,

---

[6] And neither should you be, it's one of the most surefire ways to fast-track yourself to financial stress, even if you can afford it. Stop it.
[7] 'Mo Money Mo Problems', song by The Notorious B.I.G., 1997.
[8] I'm sorry, I can't help it, it won't be my last.
[9] Yes, I've read a lot of them. Check out my six-pack.
[10] Why are you still here? Why haven't you gone out for a walk to get a carrot smoothie?

INTRODUCTION

there are also big scary banks, lots of technical jargon combined with numbers and maths which can make the difficulty of getting to grips with money almost impossible.

Well, the good news is that it's not. Understanding how to get financially fit is even simpler than getting physically fit and really boils down to one single overarching principle:

Learn to spend well.

There is only so much you can do about, and think about, how much you earn. Get or change your job. Educate yourself over many years. Marry a footballer. Win the lottery. Find out that dear departed Uncle Bob was actually a millionaire and left you some money in his will. Don't get me wrong, finding ways to get money is really important, but there are only so many ways that you can actively change your income.

What you can do, every day, is spend what money you have better, or indeed don't spend it at all. Understanding what your financial resources are (for good or bad) but more importantly making sure you deploy them effectively and in equilibrium is the secret to reaching a state of financial zen. What you'll also learn is how much of a difference doing this well will make to your finances and your mental well-being.

So how do you learn to spend well? I've set out 10 rules for how do this across two sections: 'What' and 'How':

What comprises five rules around what we need to be aware of. This is our foundation.

How are five concrete rules to help us tackle the What.[11]

To give you a sense of where we are going, I'm going to summarise the 10 rules here.[12]

---

[11] There is a final optional bonus rule for those of us who have kids, grandkids or little people we care about.
[12] But in return for me revealing the plot and the ending, I ask that you promise to read the entire book, to absorb each of the lessons and think how you could adapt your life to incorporate these rules into your life to become a financial zen master.

Introduction

WHAT

Rule 1 – Focus on your daily spend. Ignore the noise.

When it comes down to it, it's actually very simple: focus on your spending. Everything you earn you are ultimately going to spend somewhere. If you read the financial pages or look at most stuff online there is a huge amount of stuff on savings and investments which is really complex, you can ignore almost all of this. Why don't people talk about spending well? Because no-one, apart from you, makes any money from it.[13]

Rule 2 – Understand yourself.

We are all different, and the reasons why we spend what we do are all different. Work out what kind of spender you are, try and change, or learn how to manage your particular challenges.

Rule 3 – Understand others.

Almost no-one wants you to spend well, everyone wants you to spend your money: your family, your friends and social circle, banks, lenders, shops, social media, the government. By understanding the 'enemy' you can learn how to come to terms with all of the forces which consciously or unconsciously conspire to make you spend poorly.

Rule 4 – Small things matter.

Even small amounts of good spending behaviour can add up to very big changes in financial outcomes. The most basic daily improvements in spending can change your life.

Rule 5 – Master debt. Don't let it master you.

There are different kinds of debt, both good and bad[14] – work out which is which and do everything in your power to avoid or repay the bad kind.

---

[13] Well some people do talk about it to be fair. A shout out to Martin Lewis, the Money Savings Expert, and Chris and Jordan on the UK TV programme *Eat Well for Less?* For example.
[14] Like cholesterol.

INTRODUCTION

HOW

Rule 6 – Audit your spending history.

Work out exactly what you spend, where and why. Work out what your stable equilibrium spending level is so you can stick to it in a way that is permanent, sustainable and eliminates mental clutter. This is the first and most important step. Even if you stop here good things will happen.

Rule 7 – Build healthy spending habits that work for you.

Given who you are, and what you spend, what are the habits that you can adopt which work for you?

Rule 8 – How to shop.

Spend less by finding deals. It's not as hard as you think, and it's fun.

Rule 9 – Make mastering money fun.

Being in control of your money isn't a chore, it's fun. Remember that, as well as the pleasure of being in control, everything you don't spend now can be spent on something else in the future.

Build a positive connection with money. This is less about how wealthy you are, and more about how aware you are and how good you feel about yourself on a daily basis. That's a function of small habits and self-awareness.

Rule 10 – Begin investing daily.

Investing isn't complex, it's easy. It's also easy to do it regularly (in small amounts if required). When you have sorted out your spending, try and put a little bit of money aside for the future. You will feel great about it.

Bonus Rule 11 – Help your children (or young people in your life) become money maestros.

For a lot of people, anxiety about money is not just personal, it's a family thing. Spend some time getting your children financially fit and healthy, and you will feel less stressed about it yourself.[15]

---

[15] No, my parents' constant horror stories about debt and materialism didn't help me. They scared me, and probably impacted me negatively in my twenties since it put me off focusing on my finances.

That's it. The book sets each of these rules out in their own lovely chapters.

This book won't reveal any secrets of the universe, but if you follow its advice, most of which will seem like common sense, I hope it can change your life for the better. I have tried to make the rules simple in order to encourage you to start attempting to spend life well as soon as possible. Why is this so important now?

It has never been easier to spend badly. The demise of cash and the digitisation of the economy, the power of social media and marketing, the ingenuity of debt providers[16] are all factors which are making it harder for people to master their outgoings.

The world *seems* really stressful right now.[17] Let's not add to it the cost-of-living crisis, worries about geopolitics, the climate, our place in the world by layering on financial worries – sorting out one of the major sources of stress you can actually do something about is a great thing to do today.

This is a good time to save. As interest rates rise, it causes problems but also lots of opportunities. Debt is more expensive and harder to come by. Conversely savings accounts yield much better interest rates. This is when a lot of people start to curb their borrowing and begin saving or thinking about paying off their mortgages.[18] You should be part of this and get your share of assets and wealth if you can.

Finally, why not? The best part is, we can improve our spending habits dramatically without any major deterioration in our quality of life.[19] Little things add up over time – if you remove a little thing each day you barely notice it.

Let's do it.

---

[16] Buy Now Pay Later anyone? Don't make me give you my stern look, and see the chapter on debt, because that is exactly what it is.
[17] I highlight the word *seems* here – it isn't actually clear to me how bad it actually is compared to how it used to be, anyone remember the 1970s? But it certainly feels pretty awful sometimes.
[18] If they are lucky enough to be a homeowner. Another important topic for later in the book.
[19] I have learned in fact, in most cases not at all – in fact it makes everything better.

SECTION I

WHAT

'Do not save what is left after spending, but spend what is left after saving.'
> —*Warren Buffet – arguably the greatest investor in the world*

'With all due respect Warren, that's rubbish.
Save what is left after spending wisely.'
> —*Mat Megens – first-time author*

CHAPTER ONE

RULE 1: FOCUS ON YOUR DAILY SPENDING

Ignore the noise. Forget investing, forget your debts and mortgage for now. Let's start with mindful spending.

'Annual income twenty pounds, annual expenditure nineteen, nineteen, and six, result happiness. Annual income twenty pounds, annual expenditure twenty pounds ought and six, result misery.'

—Charles Dickens, *David Copperfield*

10 THINGS I ~~HATE~~ LOVE ABOUT MONEY

What I hate – Discussions on personal finance quickly divert into complicated theory and maths – it seems hugely complicated, so people ignore it or give up.

What I love – I love how being in control of your finances starts with one simple thing, mastering spending. You need to walk before you can run, and you don't ever need to run to get into good financial shape. Don't overcomplicate it. It's not about interest rates or stocks and bonds, it's about making the most of your income.

People who want to run a marathon, or become a bodybuilder or even an Olympic athlete, start with the basics.[1] The beautiful thing about the basics of fitness is for 99% of people you can stop right there and get pretty much all you need for a healthy life. What are the basics? Drink water, eat well, get your sleep, and move every day. The beauty of these really simple principles is that not only are they straightforward to achieve, but they are very easy to measure.[2] Just by measuring them regularly you will almost certainly naturally improve behaviours and feel better about yourself. You do those things, and you have the foundation for whatever excellence you want to achieve. It's simple and elegant. Money is remarkably similar.

The first rule is a change in mindset suitable for everyone. For the saver, the spender, those mired in debt, those without any debt, students, parents, retirees, working two jobs or on disability benefits. It doesn't matter who you are, this will help you. We're going to discuss a few key points.

- Most of personal finance is noise which you can ignore, at least for now.
- Be mindful of your spending because it's the most important thing you can do to improve your financial situation and happiness.

---

[1] I like comparisons to fitness because the similarities are striking and hopefully relatable. As a bonus, you might even get in better shape.
[2] That is, 2–3 l of water, 1,500–2,000 calories, 7+ hours of sleep, 10,000 steps. That sort of thing.

Rule 1: Focus on Your Daily Spending

- How much you spend is really easy to measure.[3]
- As the economy becomes more digital, it becomes increasingly harder to know how much you are spending.
- We earn over £1 million on average over our lifetimes so small changes to our behaviour can make a huge difference both whilst earning but also in retirement.

Throughout the book we are going to dig deeper into what causes bad spending and what it takes to spend well.

WHY SPENDING IS MORE IMPORTANT THAN SAVINGS

Even away from all of the benefits of feeling in control, for most people spending well is a far more important factor in financial wellness than savings or investments. Ask yourself, at first glance does this statement seem correct?

Figure 1.1 shows how much lifetime spending compares to the average pension pot in the United Kingdom.

Unbelievable, isn't it? And remember, everything you save up, ultimately you expect that you (or your loved ones) will ultimately spend.

Why don't people talk more about it? If you look around at the world today, whether that is television, social media, even your friends or family, saving and investing is typically discussed far more often than spending habits. Certainly, on a commercial level, you'll see plenty of advertisements for savings products trying to tempt you into a new account or investments offering an attractive interest rate. I'm always astounded by the sheer amount of conversations there are about moving money into accounts with

---

[3] Although it's made a lot harder if you have loads of different cards and ways to spend. Just saying.

10 THINGS I ~~HATE~~ LOVE ABOUT MONEY

Figure 1.1   Spending versus Savings

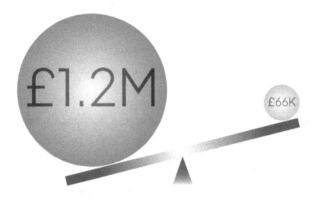

high interest rates.[4] Figure 1.2 illustrates how often you'll hear saving discussed versus mindful spending.

Compare Figure 1.2 to Figure 1.1. It seems backwards, doesn't it? But the reasons for it aren't hard to see.

No one really makes any money from people spending well. Banks (and others) like to lend you money. Shops like you to buy things. Advertisers and social media companies want to convince shops that they can make you buy stuff. Investment managers and financial advisors want you to invest in ISAs. Utilities and subscription services are delighted if you never bother to renegotiate or shop around. Even the government likes you to spend – it pushes up VAT receipts and allows them to make statements about growth.[5] Not only does no-one (apart from you) benefit from you cutting down on your posh coffee habit by one cup a day, getting rid of one of your movie subscriptions, and buying one less designer handbag a year using Buy Now Pay Later (BNPL), they actively don't want you to change your habits since it hits their financial bottom line. If you spend well, the banks will lend less, and shops will sell less. This is pervasive, the entire economy is geared around making and taking money from you, either directly, or indirectly by

---
[4] Don't get me wrong – you should absolutely do this at the first opportunity.
[5] We cover this in a lot more detail in Rule 3.

Figure 1.2   How Much We Talk about Spending and Saving[6]

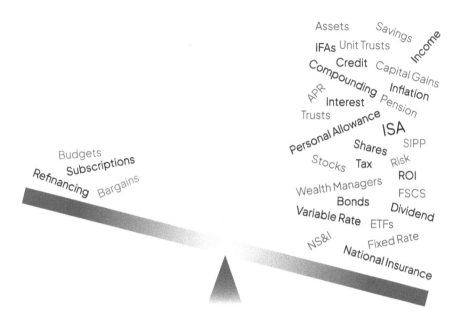

advising you about savings, getting your savings, getting you to leave too much money in your current account earning next to nothing, getting you to borrow or use BNPL, and getting you to buy and transact as much as possible. Spending less is not something shops or banks really want to encourage. Because of this, you've been on your own.[7]

For example: I find it completely bizarre how much media and personal bandwidth is spent discussing high-interest bank accounts. Of course you should put your money in one, and I'm going to encourage you to do so, but the average UK consumer has about £1,000 in their current account – 3% on this is £30 per year or to put it another way, you will make more money by cutting out one posh latte a month.[8] That's it.

Figure 1.3 shows what the balance of the discussion really should be.

---

[6] Thank you AI for your matchless ability to create word salads.
[7] Until now that is. Group hug.
[8] Or far less than a single round of drinks in the pub at an office Christmas party. It was a good night though.

Figure 1.3 What We Should Be Talking About

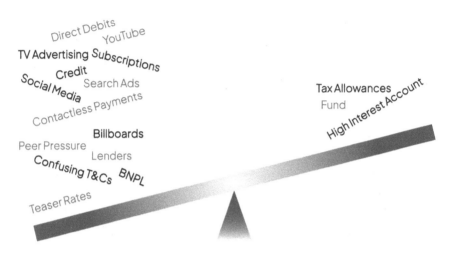

As we will see later on in Rule 10, savings and investments are really straightforward to get right, and you only have to think about it very occasionally.

It may seem odd to describe spending as complicated, at the end of the day you are just tapping your card, but the pressures surrounding doing this simple thing well are extensive. It's an odd paradox but once you understand it, and its implications, it can be truly life changing.

WHY IS SPENDING WELL EVEN HARDER NOW?

The first point to understand is that these days opportunities to spend exist everywhere. Before the internet became ubiquitous, you had to hop in your car and go into the shop. Perhaps you had to avoid the salesman coming to your door. When I was a kid, this was mostly people selling sets of encyclopedias or aerial photographs of the farm.[9] Now, every time you pick up your mobile phone, you will be presented with temptations to spend. Even though you're aware of this, I doubt everyone comprehends how invasive and pervasive this spending pressure is.

In any given day, you will come across hundreds of opportunities to buy something. You are being tempted whether you realise it or not. This constant programming becomes subconscious. And today, the friction required to spend is almost non-existent with the emergence of contactless payments. In fact, it just keeps getting easier and easier to physically spend your money. Compare the old days of getting cash out from the bank that has evolved to using an ATM; to a credit card you had to sign; to debit cards with chip and pin; to contactless and Apple/Android Pay.

Physical cash has given way to digital currency. I'm not talking about bitcoin or crypto, I'm simply referring to using credit and debit cards to transact on everyday purchases. This trend has been growing strongly and there are no signs of it slowing down. It is simply more convenient than physical cash for most consumers and handling physical cash by shops is a gigantic pain and has many risks (including being robbed or losing notes when depositing the cash).

What has the shift to digital meant for shoppers? Everything is harder and harder.

Marketing has got better and better at making you spend because they have way more data to figure you out. It is also much easier to give you tempting rewards and cashback.[10]

Lenders and banks have got better and better at making you borrow because they have more data to figure you out. They can also embed attractive lending products like BNPL directly into your digital spending journeys.

Many people now have multiple cards and multiple accounts – it's harder and harder to see how much you actually have.

---
[9] My dad bought about ten of these aerial photographs over the years and I love them now because you can see how things changed over time. Not all products sold door to door are (totally) useless.
[10] And you should take them, but only on stuff that you actually need to buy.

Physical cash has almost disappeared so it's harder and harder to work out how much you actually have (or have not) got, exactly how much you are spending when you tap your card, or put brakes on spending because most people are only dimly aware of their balance.

Imagine you had a £50 note[11] and no card, and you were going to go out for the day. You would be very careful with how you spent that £50. Every time you spent, you would get change, and you would have a new idea of how much money you have left. You would be more thoughtful about how you were planning to spend the remainder because when you are done you are done. As shown in Figure 1.4, you essentially are forced to budget because there isn't an endless supply. With digital and contactless, you have access to your entire current and savings accounts and can probably go overdrawn or into debt, thus the concept of a daily spend limit or budget is basically non-existent. More importantly, there is little feeling of loss because all you experience is a confirmation beep that the transaction was successful.[12] As a result of this, most people currently underestimate

Figure 1.4   Cash Is Physical and Visible

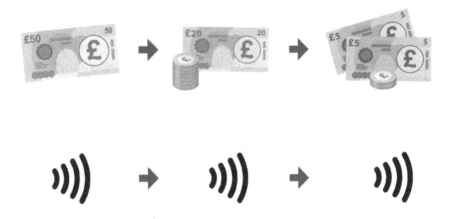

---
[11] I know it's hard to believe but yes, they still exist. I saw someone using one in a shop a few days ago and was amazed. Like seeing a Panda or other endangered species.
[12] Which let's face it, some people really enjoy.

how much they spend in a day. Trying to be in control of your spending is an increasingly tough task in a digital world, as shown in Figure 1.4.

The United Kingdom in particular, has strongly shifted to digital transactions.[13] Whether that's contactless and Apple Pay at the checkout, online shopping using your credit card, or instant money transfers to your friend, most of your financial transactions will be digital.

Why have we switched? Because digital payments are simply far more convenient, especially when one wants to transact online. Today, in an increasing number of places you can no longer use cash at all.[14]

This problem is exacerbated dramatically for young people who only know digital. Trying to understand the value and scarcity of money is difficult at the best of times, even more so when you have never even seen it.

I believe this paradigm shift is one of the most important considerations as to why many struggle to get ahead financially and why it's never been harder.[15]

WHAT IS MINDFUL SPENDING?

Mindful spending isn't the same as budgeting at all.

We don't just dive into a budget. A budget is the last step, it's about the future. Think of a budget as an accompaniment to your beautiful habits

---

[13] There has been a steady decline in the use of cash in the UK since 2012. Cash payments in 2019 were less than half those of a decade ago (Payment Systems Regulator, *Snapshot of Payments in the UK Over Time*, 2020, https://www.psr.org.uk/media/20ob5wee/payments-over-time.pdf).

[14] It's funny how London cab drivers used to insist on cash a few years ago and get quite narked if you tried to pay by card. I actually tried to pay by cash recently and the cab driver was both surprised and didn't have any change.

[15] It is interesting to note that in the last few years cash (like vinyl records) has been making a bit of a resurgence. The main hypotheses around why, relate to people preferring cash because it is easier to control spending – as in you can't spend what you haven't got. This is often called 'Jam Jar' or 'Envelope' budgeting. Some of these themes are important in the design of HyperJar.

and mindset. Without the habits and mindset, the budget just becomes a millstone around your neck which makes you feel guilty about all the things you should have been doing but failed to.

We start by simply being mindful.

Mindful is a trendy word these days. Meditating and especially meditation apps, along with holistic practices such as yoga, has brought this term to the forefront. But mindfulness and yoga doesn't need to be reserved for the dedicated practitioners of the eastern arts.

I'm hijacking 'real' mindfulness in many ways. In our case, no meditation is necessary. It's a simple concept of focusing on the present moment and not allowing anxiety to take over your thoughts.

Aside from the barrage of marketing you encounter, you will also encounter peer and social pressure.

Put another way, if we were all robots, this wouldn't even be a category. If you could program an algorithm into your brain, your spending would probably be perfect. Imagine the Perfect Spending Robot algorithm (Figure 1.5).

Step 1: Divide income into precise buckets, say: bills; groceries; entertainment; savings. These amounts are precisely calculated based on what you have historically spent, knowledge of all current and expected prices for goods and services with appropriate margins for error.

Step 2: Do all of your usual shopping precisely based on your budgeting and splitting set out above.[16]

Step 3: Somehow manage to go out drinking with your friends, shopping in a trendy store, or cruise around on Instagram without violating any of the allocations made in Step 1.

---

[16] I think we also have to assume here that all your friends, family and acquaintances are robots also (and good robots not evil killer robots, but that's for another book).

Rule 1: Focus on Your Daily Spending

Figure 1.5 A Robot Navigating Spending

Step 4: Take all of your excess income every month and allocate it perfectly between cash, your pension, and stocks and shares ISAs.

Step 5: Repeat all the steps every single day.

It's not going to happen, is it?

The fact is that spending well seems simple but it's actually pretty hard. While there is a limited set of options at any point in time, and often it's quite obvious to know what the best decision is in hindsight, the human side often takes over and makes things so difficult. Wellness and fitness have many parallels. Do you consider yourself a health or fitness expert? The average person would not. Yet the average person knows everything they need to be healthy and fit, even if they don't know how to train to become an Olympic athlete. Yet why are so many people out of shape? For the exact same reason that so many people struggle financially – it's not the knowledge, it's the psychological aspects, the societal pressures, your upbringing, your insecurities, your personality.[17] Perhaps a bit of luck plays its part but for the majority of people it comes down to simple self-discipline and your emotional state.

One of the first things that it takes to be an expert in mindful spending is to recognise that you are not a robot and cannot be perfect, just like there is no way to be perfectly fit. Too many people get frustrated when they can't get things perfectly right so don't bother at all.[18] It's like people who try to diet, or cut back on the booze, have one bad night and throw the towel in.

Spending well follows the 80/20 rule. This rule states that 20% of your efforts produces 80% of your results. In other words, focus on a small number of important things to make a big impact. Don't try for perfection. Just get clear on who you are, how you spend, how much you have and observe.

---

[17] Yes, it's the real world. What a shame.
[18] This was definitely one of my big problems in my twenties and thirties – if I couldn't do something properly, I wouldn't even bother with it. This is a perfectly good strategy for certain parts of life but is a very poor strategy for finance.

Don't worry if you make the occasional mistake, just keep at it. After a short while good habits will form and you will wonder why you were so worried in the first place.

YOU'RE ALREADY A MILLIONAIRE

Let's revisit the big ball in Figure 1.1. Yes, it is very surprising to most people, but the average lifetime earnings of a UK resident is around £1.2 million. This dwarfs the average pension pot for retirees (£66,000) and savings (£22,000).[19]

Now because we don't start off with this amount, and because we earn it over time, and each pay slip doesn't feel that big in and of itself, it's easy to not think about it, and it's easy to waste. But imagine this: you were handed £1.2 million in your early twenties and were told that this had to last you for the rest of your life. Do you think you would approach things differently?

Imagine you did the following calculation:

Divide this lifetime income into a daily number for 45 years – assuming you retire at 65 – that would give you about £70 per day to live on for your lifetime. That doesn't sound like much does it? But this would be if we spent everything and had nothing left for retirement (and I'm ignoring inflation). If we were to repeat this exercise until the average UK life expectancy of 82 years, we'd only have £53 per day. Even more challenging. See Figure 1.6.

With this £53 in mind, it starts to make you rethink almost every purchase you make. One posh coffee a day would be almost 10% of your

---

[19] Source: HyperJar (2004) *The UK's Secret Millionaires*, July, https://www.canva.com/design/DAGIwdEi-C0/K1QeYvy3sKp0c5ULAATEFA/view?utm_content=DAGIwdEi-C0&utm_campaign=designshare&utm_medium=link&utm_source=editor

Figure 1.6 How Big Amounts Can Become Small

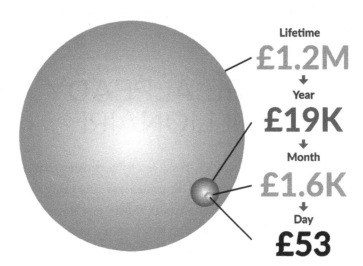

entire wealth. Conversely, saving just £5 a day could give you over £100,000 on your retirement.[20] The younger you are, the more this might hit home. If you're older, you'll have assets and debts, and it may play differently on your mind, but it may make you think back and regret certain decisions.

If you start to reframe your perspective when it comes to your income as though you are spending down a large amount, it may help you to make better decisions. If you think about £53 a day being how much the average person needs to survive on for their lives, it may help you make better decisions. We'll look into this later on in the book, so don't worry if you are unsure what to do. It's more important to understand the size and importance of your income and that every penny counts.

---

[20] Even more when you save it up properly. See Rule 4 to discover the mysteries of compounding.

RULE 1 WRAP-UP

Most of what you hear about personal finance is noise which you can ignore.

With this in mind, be mindful of your spending,[21] it's by far the most important action you can do to improve your financial situation.

Being mindful about spending is not about budgeting, it's about being aware of what you are spending and why. That's it.

A lot of the discussion about what is right for you financially is not about spending. That's because it is from people or companies who have a vested interest in divesting you of your money.

As the economy becomes more digital, it becomes increasingly harder to be mindful of your money and preserve it.

Everyone earns over £1 million on average over their lifetimes so it's very important how we manage and spend this as it can mean the difference between being financially secure or not.

The small things do add up. Good daily spending is like good daily eating and bad daily spending is like bad daily eating. The results creep up on you and it's going to ultimately help you or hurt you.

The 80/20 rule reigns supreme. That is, 20% of knowledge and activity will yield 80% of the results.

It's important to start thinking about the small things today because we can change this behaviour now.

---

[21] Pardon the pun.

CHAPTER TWO

RULE 2: UNDERSTAND YOURSELF

Money is easy, but you are complicated.

'Knowing yourself is the beginning of all wisdom'.

—Aristotle

'Be yourself; everyone else is already taken'.

—Oscar Wilde

What I hate – I hate how prescriptive and rigid most discussions about money are. We are all different and this really matters when it comes to money and especially when it comes to understanding our spending habits. **What I love** – Understanding yourself generally and how you approach life, will also lead to helping you master your spending. By understanding your strengths, but most importantly your weaknesses, you can gain more control over your emotions, impulses and interactions with others. By having this control, you will be much more confident navigating the world of money with all its traps and temptations.

For some people, maintaining physical fitness comes naturally.[1] Whether that's nature or nurture, it really depends on the person, but it's pretty rare – most people have to work at it. The world is littered with formerly fit people who have given up; people who start and fail at multiple fad diets; people with multiple unused gym memberships; people who binge eat when they are sad; people with body dysmorphia (positive or negative). This is why there is a thriving personal training industry. The key word is personal. The best trainers understand you and come up with a training protocol that's going to actually help you. One size fits all fits hardly anyone. So, you need to know all about yourself to truly make progress with your health goals, and the same is true for money.

MSPI – MAT SPENDING PERSONALITY INDICATOR

You can't even begin to master money without understanding yourself. The more you know yourself, the more you will be able to get on top of your financial life.[2]

---
[1] Me, for example. Want to go lifting?
[2] And probably other aspects of your life which is a rather nice side effect right?

Why is it so important to master your emotions and understand yourself better? Almost all of the negative behaviours which cause bad spending behaviour are really to do with personality traits: impulsiveness; overly trusting; too keen to be accepted – the list goes on.

There are thousands of research studies by experts on what makes us tick so I'm not going to reinvent the wheel here, but what I have attempted to do in this chapter is look at the major drivers of good or bad spending decisions – I think there are three. Hopefully this guided introspection will help determine your tendencies where it's relevant for money and what you can do to address this.

Because there isn't a readily common framework for indicating your spending tendencies, I've come up with my own classification and test. This is derived from common sense and thousands of data points through my fintech startup HyperJar and our millions of transactions.

I call it the *Mat Spending Personality Indicator* (MSPI).[3] It's a way of understanding your personality as it relates to money and spending. It's not super scientific as I'm not a trained psychologist, but comes from practical knowledge and data from the business I founded and my own journey. It should be used as a framework for introspection and to understand yourself better. As you delve deeper into the book, knowing your results here will help when it comes time to putting in place changes to improve your spending and wealth.

SPENDING BEHAVIOURS

I want to give some insight into how I came up with the MSPI. I started by looking at money behaviours both good and bad. The good news is, there isn't a huge list of money related behaviours. It's quite small and intuitive.

---

[3] Loosely inspired by the popular personality test called MBTI (Myers-Briggs Type Indicator). I would note that there is plenty of controversy around the effectiveness of MBTI. Personally I find the simple act of thinking about what kind of personality you are can be incredibly inciteful to navigate your way through life so the value of the test is in the process, rather than the test results.

This isn't an exact science, it's more art. It will likely confirm suspicions you have for yourself, but it will hopefully reveal some surprises too. The hardest thing about self-selecting questionnaires, however, is that there is an innate bias to answer things in a way that appears favourable to yourself. As a result, I've tried to ask questions in a way that give fewer clues as to the potential outcome. I have also considered behaviours that can go too far to an extreme and turn from good to bad. For example, saving up before you buy something, obviously a good characteristic generally. But imagine if you decided to save up the entire amount required to buy a house rather than just the deposit, you would probably be retired before you managed to buy your own home.[4] So that is an extreme example and it's the sort of nuance I want to try and explore.

Let's start with some good behaviours.

This is just a list; the behaviours are all very self-explanatory.

- Saving up before buying something.
- Sleeping on it before large purchases (or using some other thought process).
- Openly discussing financial topics of concern with close friends and family.
- Being clear about understanding the terms for a service before you pay for it.
- Being clear about what you expect from someone if you were to lend them money.
- Having goals in the future and saving for them.
- Buying things that you will actually use and enjoy.
- Not chasing sales, being deliberate in terms of what you buy.
- Understanding your subscriptions and renewal dates.

---

[4] And a home is usually a great investment – see Rule 10. Plus, based on nothing but anecdotal evidence, I think owning your own home is often a huge net positive when it comes to feeling financially healthy.

- Price comparison shopping and getting best value for any purchase.
- Researching your purchases so you don't regret them.

Let's look at some bad behaviours.

Many of these can be considered the opposite of what is listed above. I'll try to frame them somewhat differently though.

- Buying things impulsively.
- Not discussing financial topics with anyone, even when in distress.
- Buying services without understanding the terms and contract (whether due to shyness, apathy or laziness).
- Using debt for purchasing things that depreciate.[5]
- Spending all your money, especially when you get a bit more than normal (for example, a bonus).
- Letting any contract auto-renew (this could be insurance, Sky, broadband provider, etc.).
- Lending money to friends or family.
- Paying full price for most discretionary items you purchase.
- Regularly throwing out unused food from the fridge each week.
- Regularly buying water or soda from a convenience store, and other single size items.
- Supermarket shopping when you're hungry and buying too much food.
- Buying multi-packs to get a better price even if you only need one of the items (worse for non-consumables such as plastic containers or stationery, for example).

As you can see there are a limited set of behaviours that can have profound impact on your spending, and they are all pretty easy to identify if you focus on being mindful.

---
[5] Especially items which depreciate by more than half their value the moment you leave the shop. Like fast fashion.

SPENDING PERSONALITIES

Here we go. The foundation of the MSPI involves three personality axes which most closely relate to spending situations. Each of these three axes is really a spectrum upon which someone will mostly lie.[6]

(1) **Understanding** – An ability and willingness to be aware of your financial situation, but more importantly, your spending habits. There are many reasons why someone may not be aware of their money situation, from ignorance to fear but the reasons why are less important. The tendency to be aware or not is what matters for now. Later we'll look at the why and how we can change this to become beneficial.

Spectrum: **Clueless** to **Informed**

(2) **Receptiveness** – A tendency to accept what you are told versus questioning and debating. It includes your comfort level with asking for money owed or getting more details regarding a contract or offer. Reasons for this may involve social discomfort, upbringing or general attitude.

Spectrum: **Accepting** to **Defiant**

(3) **Impulsiveness** – This is someone's tendency to make quick unconsidered decisions versus careful thought-out decisions. This is mostly due to someone's innate personality and upbringing but sometimes it really is simply a blind spot when it comes to shopping.[7]

Spectrum: **Reckless** to **Thoughtful**

---

[6] But honestly, in my experience it's more binary than you think. People are either pretty good, or absolutely hopeless.

[7] One of the most thoughtful organised people I know, a senior lawyer, has the most extraordinary inability to go into a shop without walking out clutching handfuls of bags full of expensive goodies. She can afford it, that's not the point here, she is a remarkably reckless shopper. I bet you know some yourself. Or is it you?

Rule 2: Understand Yourself

With these three axes and six traits, we can now derive our eight spending personality types. The difference between these types and most personality tests is that these are moveable, not permanently fixed to your personality. Because of this, multiple types may resonate with you depending on the spending situation you are faced with. We start with a questionnaire to determine your default indicator, which is the one that affects you most.

THE MSPI SURVEY

Twenty-four statements are all that lie between you and the secrets of the universe.[8]

For each of these I use a 1–5 scale where **1 is absolutely not** and **5 is absolutely yes**.

Binary yes/no questions are often too difficult to answer as life rarely presents us with simple yes/no choices.

For example, the question 'Do you enjoy Sundays?' might require a complicated answer. You might enjoy the day off, but you might have the Sunday Scaries and be a bit sad about having to go to work the next day. So maybe you give it a 3. This is better than Yes or No. The 1–5 scale tries to capture nuance.

Respond to the statements in Tables 2.1–2.3 with your score between 1 and 5. Don't worry about trying to make the answer exact, just go with your first instinct. There are eight statements in three different categories. Later we'll add up our scores.

---

[8] Okay maybe that's an exaggeration. Twenty-four statements to ponder for a little bit of fun and to help guide us in later rules when we look at building good habits (PS: the answer is 42).

10 THINGS I ~~HATE~~ LOVE ABOUT MONEY

Table 2.1 Understanding

Number	Statement	Score (1–5)
1	I know roughly what the price of my shopping is before the cashier rings it up on the till	
2	I know how much money I have in the bank	
3	I'm happy discussing money and finance with other people	
4	I know what a percentage is and how to calculate an APR	
5	I know how much debt I have and how to calculate the interest	
6	Working out how to split a bill holds no fear for me	
7	I'm happy filling out the information in forms	
8	I look at my bank statements each month	
TOTAL SCORE		

Table 2.2 Receptiveness

Number	Statement	Score (1–5)
9	When I lend someone money, I find it uncomfortable asking them for the money back	
10	When I go about my day, I always follow all rules and social conventions and rarely break them even if convenient and no one will know	
11	When my insurance and other contracts expire, I almost always automatically renew	
12	I always pay asking price in shops or when I buy things from other people	
13	If there's a dispute with a friend, I tend to be agreeable to avoid an argument	
14	When I become part of a new social group, I go along with consensus and rarely speak up	
15	At work or school, I will typically show agreement with my boss or teacher (even if I disagree)	
16	I rarely or never carefully check my receipts or online basket when I shop	
TOTAL SCORE		

Rule 2: Understand Yourself

Table 2.3   Impulsiveness

Number	Statement	Score (1–5)
17	When I really want something in the shops, I will just buy it	
18	When I shop online, I rarely price comparison shop	
19	I often use credit to buy larger purchases	
20	I usually finance larger purchases like cars or furniture	
21	When friends suggest going out, I almost always agree	
22	I usually buy the most expensive iPhone/technology	
23	I am influenced by social media influencer product recommendations	
24	My friends and family can easily convince me to buy things	
TOTAL SCORE		

Now I need you to work out the following simple maths.

Add up the following point totals. Each bucket will have a minimum of 8 and a maximum of 40:

Understanding (add the sum total of Statements 1 through 8)
- If you scored 8–24, you're Closed (**C**).
- If you scored 25–40, you're Open (**I**).

Receptiveness (add the total of Statements 9 through 16)
- If you scored 8–24, you're Defiant (**D**).
- If you scored 25–40, you're Accepting (**A**).

Impulsiveness (add the total of Statements 17 through 24)
- If you scored 8–24, you're Thoughtful (**T**).
- If you scored 25–40, you're Reckless (**R**).

You now have your three-letter designation. Go back, check which label you have been identified with and see if it matches what you expected it would be. Let's discuss the designations and draw some conclusions.[9]

---
[9] Possibly unfairly – like I said, this is an exercise in getting to know yourself rather than an attempt to put you in a box.

CAR (Clueless/Accepting/Reckless) = Nightmare

A **Nightmare** has all the worst traits that make for an awful spender. No interest in money or understanding their own financial peril, free with their spending, both on their own behalf and also on the whims of others around them. The problem here is that the situation is so bad that it becomes self-reinforcing, where someone just throws the towel in and gives up. So it gets worse. Don't give up, get help.

CAT (Clueless/Accepting/Thoughtful) = Pleaser

A **Pleaser** is someone who finds dealing with or talking about money distasteful or uncomfortable. They will never negotiate, question a price or tell Sky they're leaving after the contract ends because of their lousy offers. These are people who tend to pay for everything and never ask for anything in return and get taken advantage of.[10]

CDR (Clueless/Defiant/Reckless) = Ostrich

An **Ostrich** is someone who knows full well that they should change gas supplier, cancel Sky, stop being silly, and feel that they have solved the problem – but haven't actually done it.[11] But they also have their head in the sand. They simply refuse to look at their finances at all and have no idea what their balance is. They are almost pathologically proud about their lack of understanding. As a coping mechanism they often boast about it (but secretly they are really depressed about it). Get a grip.

CDT (Clueless/Defiant/Thoughtful) = Hoarder

A **Hoarder** will buy anything which they think offers value regardless of whether they need it or not.[12] It can be almost a medical problem (like an overeater, a hoarder is an over-spender and what they spend on doesn't need to be expensive).

---

[10] This could be due to generosity or cowardice. You decide.
[11] This reminds me of a joke that maybe only nerds like me will find humorous. A physicist, engineer and mathematician are asked to define Pi. The mathematician says Pi is the number expressing the relationship between the circumference of a circle and its diameter. The physicist says Pi is 3.1415927 plus or minus 0.000000005. The engineer says Pi is about 3.
[12] For example, a friend's dad has three portable gas burners bought from the Lidl middle isle. This is nothing compared to some people – watch Stacey Solomon on the excellent TV programme *Sort Your Life Out*.

IAR (Informed/Accepting/Reckless) = Coveter

A **Coveter** has to have something as good as or better than their neighbour or friends. Hence the expression 'Keeping up with the Joneses'. A Coveter is almost always going to overspend, because there is always someone out there with more money than you.[13] This is a huge problem for children in the age of social media.

IAT (Informed/Accepting/Thoughtful) = Hermit

A hermit knows precisely how money works and they are careful with it. Even so, since they tend to be socially shy, they are always getting taken advantage of by friends, service providers and others. Very often they retreat into their shells and avoid situations where this occurs since it will make them unhappy. Calling up to renegotiate a contract, or bargaining makes them come out in a sweat, so they never do it.

IDR (Informed/Defiant/Reckless) = Dopamine Addict

A **Dopamine Addict** is someone who simply gets pleasure from buying stuff. A friend of mine has this problem – it's like comfort eating. But they are also someone who must have the most expensive thing, not because someone else has it, but because they must have the best. See fashion. See people who sort goods on Amazon by price and buy the most expensive one. See the millionaires who only eat lobster, sushi and steak and drink Bordeaux and never have a curry because it's too cheap. It becomes a social status. And this type of social status can impoverish even the wealthiest (any athletes or movie stars come to mind?).

IDT (Informed/Defiant/Thoughtful) = Zen

Zen is when you achieve balance after you follow the rules in this book. This is the best combination of traits. You understand money, you don't waste it on yourself or others and buy the things you need (or want) when you actually need them. Congratulations.

---

[13] Unless you are Elon Musk. But would you want to swap places with him?

Note that being thoughtful about money doesn't mean I'm saying you shouldn't have fun – this is a key part of what money (and the spending of it) is for. Don't be so focused on saving that you wear a hair shirt every day and have almost no fun, dying rich with no friends.[14]

That's it, eight indicators shown in Figure 2.1. These aren't black and white designations. People can exhibit aspects of each. Each axis lies on a

Figure 2.1   The Eight Indicators

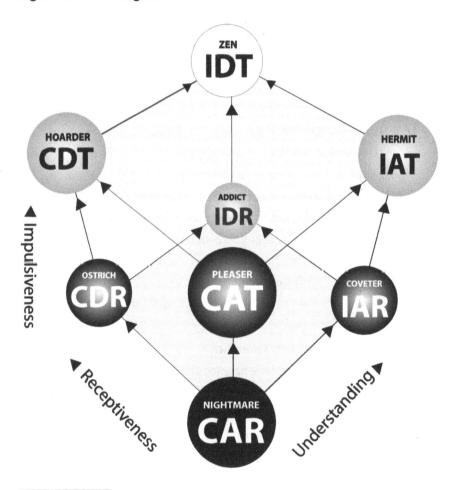

---
[14] Exaggeration for dramatic emphasis.

Rule 2: Understand Yourself

spectrum and even then, will not always be the same depending on circumstances and situations.

WHAT DOES IT ALL MEAN?

The quiz might be interesting or even entertaining, but what does this all mean?

I mentioned at the start of this chapter how the popular psychological tests try to determine your personality and give you a label. That label is predominantly fixed, and you have to learn how to deal with it because you won't be changing it. My test is quite different. I look at habits and tendencies that can be changed.

Now your MSPI type has come about because of many factors – upbringing; personality; life experiences – but like the physical fitness, you can do something about it.

Anyone can become fitter, if you understand yourself and what blocks you from doing the simple things you need to. For some people it comes naturally, but for almost everyone it's possible. If you understand yourself, you can learn how to get yourself to a place where you can become fit.

It is exactly the same thing with spending. You can either try and change category (which is hard), or by understanding who you are you can modify your behaviour accordingly (more straightforward).

Let me give an example to explain.

Let's take a random MSPI, Coveter (IAR) and see how we can start to move towards a state of financial Zen (IDT), our ultimate goal.

So in this case our lovely assistant is currently Informed, Accepting and Reckless. They understand their finances but are constantly spending money either on, or because of, other people and their opinions. This is a pretty stressful place to be.[15]

---

[15] Spend in haste, repent at leisure.

Meanwhile, to achieve Zen requires shifting to being more Defiant and more Thoughtful, essentially addressing two of the three indicators.

What does this mean exactly? Our friend knows exactly what they are doing, so it isn't financial ignorance. It requires a shift to becoming more critical and curious when it comes to money situations. What kind of questions should they be asking every time they look at their statement and the payments that they have made with their tendency to be Accepting?

- Who am I trying to impress and why?
- Why did I let my friends talk me into doing that?
- Why haven't I got rid of this subscription?
- Why haven't I changed my supplier?
- Why did I pay the bill not split it?
- We agreed to split the bill, why didn't I ask for the money back?

And what about when thinking about being Reckless? Questions like:

- Why did I buy that?
- Am I happy I spent that money?
- Could I have waited before buying it?
- Why didn't I try and see if there was a better price?
- Could I actually afford it?
- Did I buy it on credit?
- Did I really need that extra Martini?

In terms of Understanding and being Clueless, it's so important it has its own section – Rule 5.

But this underlines the key point. The only thing that you really have to do is make sure that you observe yourself and be honest with yourself about how and why you spend what you spend.

Sometimes the act of changing habits will just occur organically as you repeatedly observe poor spending habits. Sometimes it requires a bit of deliberate practice and training: but it really is possible to overcome shyness; be more questioning of uncomfortable situations; ensure that what you sign up for is what you expect.

To the extent that you simply cannot change behaviours then you really need to think about changing your environment: spend less time with friends who encourage you to make foolish financial decisions; don't look at the middle isle in Lidl; don't go to Oxford Street after a boozy lunch.[16] It really is possible to build in friction or guardrails to help manage spending.

This can all be accomplished despite inherent biases. Become aware of your triggers when you spend. Devise bigger goals that motivate you to stop seeking a dopamine rush from shopping.

MY JOURNEY – FROM NIGHTMARE TO ZEN

I'm going to use myself as an example here. If you recall, I set out my background in the Prologue – so why exactly was I a Nightmare?

Acceptance

My situation:

- I am highly financially literate and spent my entire day working on complex problems to do with money, risk and investments.
- Despite this, in fact probably because of this, I didn't take my work home with me. I just assumed that it wasn't a problem, or that it was something I could deal with later in life because I was earning good money.[17]
- I am also a perfectionist, so unless I can do something very well, I tend not to bother to do it at all. I simply didn't accept the 80/20 rule, that

---
[16] Or if you do, don't go into Selfridges. Or if you go into Selfridges give your credit cards to a friend first.
[17] This is a problem for many people. If you know there is a solution to a problem, you try to solve it.

getting a grip on spending is an end in and of itself, rather than being the best spender/investor ever. This is a real problem for many people.

As a result:

- I spent very little time looking at my personal finances or my spending.
- I spent zero time thinking about my financial equilibrium and balancing my income and expenditure, this was especially bad since my love of start-ups and jobs with performance-related pay meant that my income varied enormously over the years. My expenditure also changed dramatically as my family grew, but I simply never sat down and worked it all out. I just mentally kicked the can down the road.
- I didn't get involved in any form of savings, personal investment or buying a property.

Authority

My situation:

- I have always been good at finding the best price for everything.
- I'm fearless about negotiating.
- So what is my problem? It's other people.
- I'm simply terrible about saying no to family and close friends. I don't like confrontation, or more properly, I don't like disappointing people I know.

As a result:

- I was never good about talking to other people about getting on top of their spending – I always felt it was too preachy.
- I was always far too willing to agree to, and fund, requests from family and friends, without stopping to think about why. I just wanted to make people happy.

- People always assumed, because of my job history, that I was richer than I actually was. I never stopped to point out that this was not actually true.
- Rich people's things – cars, private school fees and healthcare, fancy holidays, memberships – are really really expensive.
- As a result, my income was my own, but expenditure was social – this made it even more opaque and difficult to manage and get wrong.

Impulsiveness

My situation:

- I'm not actually a big spender most of the time.
- I'm not into fashion or fine dining.
- I don't feel any need to keep up with the Joneses.
- But I have three weaknesses when it comes to money: cars, motorbikes and technology.[18]
- I would love all three even if there was no-one left on the planet, but my problem was definitely exacerbated by my best friends. They shared my weaknesses and had the funds to indulge them.

As a result:

- In my (relative) youth I spent a ridiculously high proportion of my spare cash on cars, motorcycles and the next new gadget.
- It never occurred to me that I should save any of it – I had no concept of delayed gratification.
- I never bothered to use my spare cash for more what I perceived as more 'boring' uses, such as funding a pension or saving up for a house deposit.

---

[18] I know, I know. A classic nerd. Why on earth did I need to pick such expensive weaknesses?

10 THINGS I ~~HATE~~ LOVE ABOUT MONEY

So why did I change? Because I had to. I decided to leave my lovely well-paid job[19] to do something entrepreneurial again. My income plummeted overnight. Unfortunately my wife shared my love of entrepreneurship and ran her own small business. She also shared my love of children[20] and my love of nice cars. There was literally no way I could see a way forward financially without doing a bit of rapid growing up.

I finally had to focus on really understanding spending, both for myself and my family. We prioritised what we actually needed rather than what we wanted.[21] My word, we spent money on a lot of nonsense – that all stopped.

As far as my interactions with other people, I simply learned to say 'no, I can't afford that'.[22] I'll be honest, it was really tough initially, I think we are conditioned to believe that somehow spending lots of money makes you seem successful, fun and generous, with the obvious corollary that controlling your spending makes you unsuccessful, boring and miserly. This is complete nonsense of course but it's pervasive.

Becoming thoughtful not reckless was simply something I had to do. I certainly learned from my parents that getting into debt is a really bad idea, so with that hard line I wouldn't cross we simply didn't have the resources to be reckless with.

You know what? Nothing really material changed – sure, our holidays weren't quite as flashy, our house wasn't as nice as if might have been, but it was fine. The posh restaurant visits were less frequent or less posh, but it was amazing how much fat we managed to cut from our spending without making any measurable difference to what really mattered.

What really did change was my relationship with money. It got better, I felt happier because I was in control of it. Every time I didn't waste money

---

[19] As a partner in an asset management firm set up by my friend Paul. I must have done something right though – I convinced him to leave and join me when I embarked on my HyperJar adventure.
[20] Four kids. Reckless?
[21] No new motorbike for me. For now. Let's see if anyone buys this book.
[22] Most importantly to my family – it's hard, but when explained properly it can be done.

it made me happy. It's different from dieting, you deny yourself a cheeseburger you just feel hungry; you don't buy yourself an expensive meal, you have a hundred pounds left in your pocket.

The other really interesting fact that really surprised me was it wasn't just about how I was feeling about the present, it was how I was feeling about the future. You lead a certain lifestyle with a certain cost to it, and not surprisingly you want that to continue. When you think about how much you are going to need going forward it can be overwhelming. By getting in control of my spending, and by spending less, I felt much more confident about the future, and it is amazing how much small amounts of savings add up (see the next chapter) and how knowing that you need less can make you so much happier.[23]

As I grew older and wiser,[24] I was able to work on my inherent money weaknesses and turn them into strengths. Because MSPI isn't your innate personality, but your spending tendencies, you have the ability to get better through reflection and practice. I'm an introvert and always will be. But both introverts and extroverts can negotiate well, they just may feel differently about it and approach it in a different manner. What matters are the actions we take in the real world. Each of us has to adjust in a personal way to ensure we take the best actions when it comes to our money. We're going to really get into this in later chapters.

MOOD-BASED SPENDING

Your mood, positive or negative, can lead to bad spending outcomes. Depressed by a bad day at work? A bit of comfort shopping perhaps? Elated

---

[23] I think a lot of entrepreneurs feel this way. Living on vapours for a while is a little like intermittent fasting. How much do you really need? I suggest (if you are one of the strange people reading all these footnotes) that you read the Fisherman's Parable.
[24] Maybe. A little.

by your football team winning a match? Time to put your card behind the bar at the pub. Drunk whilst in charge of an Amazon account? That's interesting, when exactly did I buy this novelty item?

Mood changes caused by either situations or life or substances can lower your inhibitions or create anxiety. When your inhibitions are lowered and your mind chemistry is altered, you're more likely to indulge and be susceptible to impulses.

I'm not suggesting you don't drink or have fun.[25] But you might need to incorporate some circuit breakers in your life if you know you're prone to mood based spending. Some ideas around the theme:

- When you go out drinking use a prepaid card set to a certain limit that you can't exceed or take cash.
- Tell yourself firmly that you will wait 24 hours before you make that impulse purchase so you can see if it's actually about your state of mind.
- Don't drink and shop!
- Basically binge shopping, just like binge drinking and binge eating is a thing.[26] Recognise it, understand it, and try to build safeguards and not rely on self-discipline as much as possible.

MONEY AND LIFE

Money and life overlap all the time, I'm sure lots of us don't like this fact but unfortunately it's reality. In this chapter we've attempted to drill down into

---

[25] Quite the reverse, you are going to have to use all the money saved after reading this book for something. It might as well be entertaining.

[26] There is research showing a correlation between sunny weather and spending more money by consumers: K.B. Murray, F. Di Muro, A. Finn and P.T.L. Popkowski Leszczyc (2010) 'The Effect of Weather on Consumer Spending', *Journal of Retailing and Consumer Services*, https://papers.ssrn.com/sol3/papers.cfm?abstract_id=1657977

your personality to try and get a sense of how you are with money. Unlike a personality test, these indicators are moveable or manageable. This can be achieved by stopping bad habits and building good habits in their place. Your bad habits and mistakes don't define you. If you focus on them they are a path to helping you to improve more quickly. The more honestly we confront ourselves, the faster this can happen.

Later in the book, we'll look at tangible steps that we'll take to make and break habits to help you to reach a state of financial Zen, namely becoming more Open, Defiant and Thoughtful.

It's always about balance and the goal isn't to live on the extreme edge. It's more important to be aware of qualities that will lead to successful habits and then put into place actions to help us reach equilibrium more easily.

RULE 2 WRAP-UP

Money and personality go hand in hand. It's impossible to optimise spending and reduce your life anxiety without understanding your personality. In this chapter we attempted to drill down into our own money personalities.

- Understand who you are, and with it the money challenges you are going to face.
- Ask yourself, can you move yourself away from being a Nightmare towards a state of financial Zen. It's at most three steps, for most people it's one or two.
- At the very least you have to work on your Understanding, moving from Clueless to Informed. You can understand money, it's not complex – the rest of the book covers this off in detail.
- For everything else, if you can't change you either need to: get advice; ask for help; or develop coping mechanisms such as removing yourself

from situations where you are in danger of being reckless or overly receptive.
- Our indicators are not who we are. They describe us. Because they describe us, our description can change if we put in the work and improve our habits. But knowing our tendencies will help us know what habits we need to build to get to that perfect place.

CHAPTER THREE

RULE 3: UNDERSTAND OTHERS

Your relationship with other people has a huge impact on your money. Master it.

'I don't like to commit myself about heaven and hell – you see, I have friends in both places.'

—*Mark Twain*

'Too many people spend money they haven't earned, to buy things they don't want, to impress people they don't like.'

—*Will Smith*

What I hate – Thinking about spending well is a lonely pursuit. Almost no one will be interested in helping you do it. Quite the reverse, people and companies are actively interested in you spending badly. Many of the descriptive words for someone who is careful with their money are pejorative rather than admiring. Why?

What I love – You can become wealthier and happier just by understanding your friends and the environment around you. Humans are social creatures, and your money is an integral part of this. Whether it's the influence your social network has on your financial life or the places you shop at trying to get as much of your money as possible, your environment plays an important role.

BANKS

Banks make money when you:

- Leave lots of money with them, which they are subsequently allowed to lend.
- Leave lots of money with them in low interest-rate accounts. They love it if you are foolish enough to leave large balances in current accounts which earn very little money.[1]
- Borrow money for good things like buying a house.
- Borrow money for bad things like buying a handbag. Even better.
- Don't bother refinancing loans at cheaper rates when you have the option to do so.
- Accidentally go overdrawn and pay penalty rates.
- Travel abroad and pay for things without thinking about how expensive the exchange rates are.[2]

---

[1] Especially a problem for non-digitally literate people, for example pensioners.
[2] A classic case of complexity allowing people to take advantage.

This is their business model:

- You are probably familiar with teaser rates – initial attractive rates that revert to something less attractive – are a function of the industry and without them banks would lose business.
- Like the scorpion and the frog parable, they're not evil, it's what they were designed to do from the beginning.[3]

A good spender:

- Avoids debt unless absolutely necessary, and refinances it as soon as it makes sense.
- Only keeps amounts in current accounts required to do day-to-day spending.
- Never goes overdrawn.
- Pays almost nothing for spending abroad – because you don't need to.

Banks don't find this kind of customer very attractive.

SAVINGS COMPANIES

Savings companies make money when you:

- Pay them for advice.
- Pay them to set up stuff like pensions for you.
- Pay them to manage your money for you.

This is their business model:

- They want to give you as much advice as possible.

---

[3] A scorpion wants to cross a river, but it cannot swim. It sees a frog and asks if the frog will carry him across. The frog is nervous because he is worried the scorpion will sting him. The scorpion reassures the frog, telling him that why would he sting him because if he did, they would both drown and that would not be good for either of them. The frog agrees with this logic and agrees to carry the scorpion across the river. As they are halfway across the river, the scorpion stings the frog! They are now both doomed as the frog begins to drown with the scorpion on its back. The dying frog, confused, asks the scorpion, 'Why did you sting me, now we're both going to die?' The scorpion replies, 'I'm sorry but it's my nature, I couldn't help it'.

10 THINGS I ~~HATE~~ LOVE ABOUT MONEY

- They want to do as much 'management' as possible and charge you nice big fees for doing it.

A good spender:

- Requires very little ongoing advice.
- Seeks out the lowest fees possible on savings products.
- Doesn't move money between savings products very often.

Savings companies don't find this kind of customer very attractive.

SHOPS AND MERCHANTS

Shops make money when you buy their stuff – simple as that.

A good spender:

- Doesn't spend as much as an impulsive or accepting personality type.
- Doesn't buy crap.
- Shops around.
- Rarely spends the full price.
- Never buys on credit if it can possibly be avoided.
- Often buys second hand.

Lots of shops still love you because you still buy stuff – but they are going to try as hard as possible to change your habits. That is why the marketing industry and social media are so huge.

UTILITIES

Utilities[4] make money when you:

- Pay for services from them.
- Pay for services from them that you don't actually use, and they don't need to supply.

---
[4] I include subscription services for TV in this definition. I mean, Game of Thrones? Come on.

- Don't renegotiate at the end of any teaser rates (similar to teaser rates on loans and savings accounts with banks).
- Don't shop around or switch.

A good spender:

- Only pays for what they actually use.
- Renegotiates and shops around all the time.

Utilities don't find this kind of customer very attractive at all. In fact, for some companies, a good spender is a loss-making customer.

To summarise, most companies that you deal with want you to be a mindless not a mindful spender. Not very helpful is it?

FAMILY AND FRIENDS (OR ARE THEY?)

Lastly, but most importantly, let's talk about the elephant in the room,[5] your friends and family. Friends might be a misnomer when it comes to money, as we'll soon find out. There are many situations where money is involved, and your friends don't necessarily have your best interests at heart. This doesn't mean they're out to get you. Most awkward friend money situations involve people who are trying to sort their own problems, unaware of how their demands may affect you. So, their friendship is genuine and sincere, and that is what makes it so difficult.

In the early 2000s I was living near Boston and started dating a woman. I'll call her Bea.[6] Bea and I were in very different places in our lives. I was single, childless and flush with cash, having both a very good salary and having cashed out some shares in my previous startup. I was lucky. But having no dependents,

---
[5] Or down the pub.
[6] Not her real name.

and no debt, life was almost too easy. My life felt strangely meaningless when I didn't have to worry about money. I met Bea at the gym, and she asked me out on a date. She was absolutely insistent and wanted to treat me. She picked me up in a new Lincoln[7] and took me to a nice restaurant. When it was time to pay, she again insisted on paying and pulled out a huge wad of cash, paying the bill with her crisp American dollars. I came home that evening impressed with how much effort she made and her insistence on treating me and thinking she was financially well off. It turns out, this wasn't the case at all. Bea had a job and earned decent money, but she had accrued debt over many years. This debt was spread over multiple credit cards and loans, and she was paying exorbitant interest rates, well over 20%. Her total debt was over $10,000 across eight different accounts and interest was her fastest growing expense. She would use cash because she could no longer get a credit card and was on the road to becoming unbanked. Seeing this situation and seeing some obvious mistakes, I tried to help her. This was within weeks of our first date. I was in a mode where I felt like I had to help even though we had just started dating. The first thing I thought was she needed to consolidate her debt into a single obligation and at a much better interest rate. As I started this process, it was becoming extremely complicated and then I had an idea. I had plenty of money sitting in my bank account doing nothing. I thought why don't I just give Bea an interest-free loan to help pay off all these debts and sort it out that way. I lent her around $10,000 and we made a payment plan over 5 years. Something like that. She would now have reasonable monthly payments, and she could financially start over.

You can probably guess what happened next. Within a few months we broke up, it definitely wasn't a relationship meant to be! She had been making payments while we were dating and as we broke up amicably, she endeavoured to keep repaying her loan. Within a few months, the payments stopped. She

---

[7] For those who don't know, a Lincoln was/is Ford's luxury brand in the United States. So, it would try to compete with German cars or luxury Japanese cars like Lexus.

Figure 3.1 Social Pressure – It All Adds Up

didn't completely ignore me. She was about to get some big work with an agency in NYC so would be able to pay me back soon. But the payments never happened. Once the payments stopped, they stopped forever. And my $10,000? I wrote it off and moved on. There's a very simple lesson here by the way:

NEVER LEND MONEY TO FRIENDS AND FAMILY.

You can give money to friends and family, but never be their bank. It's dangerous territory. If a bank won't lend them money, there's likely a good reason why. And if you need your money back, you're taking some serious risk. Either give a friend money, or help them get a loan from a bank, but don't be the bank.

I've come up with four social categories shown in Figure 3.1 that often trip people up when it comes to friends and family and money.

These include:

1. Pressure to participate.
2. Social status.
3. Overcoming shyness.
4. Being a yes-person.

10 THINGS I ~~HATE~~ LOVE ABOUT MONEY

Let's talk about what these social categories mean and then we'll look at ways to prevent adverse situations from harming us and our money.

PRESSURE TO PARTICIPATE

You've all been here before. The office is going out for lunch and want you to join in.[8] Your best friend is coming to town, and he wants Wimbledon centre court tickets. You're out for dinner and the group want to get the most expensive bottle of wine. It could even be something longer term, like the school ski trip that your child must go on because her friends are going.

This is real and it happens almost every day and people can tend to normalise it and soon accept a pattern of reluctant compliance.

This is especially hard for teenagers and young people who are trying to find their place socially. Or people who have just started work at a new company or have moved to a new town. You want to make friends; you want to have friendly relationships; the best thing to do is socialise. But the reality is, not everyone has the same financial resources so it can be almost impossible to align the comfortable amount of spend. This also extends to the wealthy. Perhaps you are well off and can afford an annual ski trip to Verbier. But your friend has a private jet and a personal chef in the chalet he owns.[9] In this case when you plan to buy wine, the expectation might be something beyond your already impressive budget. It's all relative.

Let's look at some examples.

Company gift pools for employees leaving or celebrating events can be a problem. The person organising will sincerely think they're doing a nice gesture but often the employees constantly being asked to donate can feel pressured, especially ones on lower wages.

---
[8] Even though you packed your lunch.
[9] I took this example from a true story I know of. The lives of others can be very entertaining.

This pressure also happens with charitable giving. Charitable giving is hugely important for many people but this is an area where it's particularly easy to feel guilt and to pull you off track with your finances and spending. You see this often on the street with hired people canvasing strangers to donate. These donations are often subscriptions, not just a single donation, so this can really add up. Think about charities as businesses – some are poorly managed, and some are managed excellently so the funds you donate may or may not go to the cause you have been led to believe they are trying to support. My advice on this is simple: never donate to any charity under duress or impulsively. If you feel uncomfortable saying no, you can simply inform them that you always do your own extensive research on a charity in your own time before you make your decision. That's it. End of discussion. You should never feel pressured to give any money to anyone.

Social pressure is a big deal. A great example of this is parent groups at schools. Teacher gifts, parent helper gifts, birthday presents for other kids[10] – the requests can seem endless. I think gifts and gestures are great but across someone's life there can be dozens and dozens of requests to chip in for people you may have no real relationship with. On top of taking care of your own responsibilities it can get overwhelming and have a negative impact on your financial life and be really stressful. Wouldn't it be great if individuals simply made a choice to buy a gift or not? This is an area where less organisation is better (in my opinion).

How about your social life? Maybe you like to go out drinking with your mates.[11] Each person takes turns buying rounds, that's fair. But does everyone drink the same amount? Likely not. Does it matter if someone buys an extra round? Not a big deal. But over months and years, this all adds up. Obviously it would be better if everyone simply paid for what they

---

[10] My four children have lots of friends. I wish they were as introverted as me.
[11] Something which I rarely do as it happens.

drunk or ate. This perfection is not possible though, so how do you find the balance?[12]

There are a few things you can do to lessen this impact on your spending. You could surround yourself with the type of people who will motivate you to be your best self and provide situations you are comfortable with – but even better is to become confident and *just say no* if that is how you feel. You will be respected, and true friends would embrace your differences. It's like going to the pub and not drinking. This is really okay. No one cares anymore, they truly don't. And if they do care, they have the problem, not you.

If you know certain situations put you in a very difficult place for whatever reason, and just saying no is not realistic, then try your best to avoid them. It's okay to not go to the pub because you're worried you will buy too many rounds. But more importantly, tell your friends the truth! A true friend cares about you, even if you're a weirdo! In fact, they probably like you because you're a weirdo. Just be honest. Life becomes so much easier when you just speak your mind and don't try to live up to any social pretences. Ideally you can figure out a way to socialise and spend what you want, but that will take some finessing and discipline to achieve. If you're still feeling uncomfortable or just don't want to discuss certain things then take a break – for a while at least.

Get comfortable making decisions that are best for you and don't feel ashamed doing so. The more you do this, the easier it gets. It's better to try to avoid uncomfortable situations than it is to practise extreme self-discipline. Every human has a breaking point so try not to test it.[13]

---

[12] No, making sure you drink and eat more than everyone else isn't the answer. Remember I'm a qualified personal trainer.

[13] This applies to so many situations from relationships to anger management. It's okay and smart to avoid things you know will be difficult for you to manage.

SOCIAL STATUS – DON'T TRY TO KEEP UP WITH THE JONESES

In case you don't know, 'keeping up with the Joneses' refers to people and families buying things and spending money in order to create an appearance of status and wealth similar to their neighbours (the Joneses). This concept is really universal across geography, age and social status, whether it's billionaires duelling with each other for who has the biggest yacht or children wanting the same Paw Patrol backpack their friend has. It's simply human nature to want to compete for attention based on our lifestyles and the things we own.

Of course, it's all about relativity. It's usually much more fun to be a big fish in a small pond than a small fish in a big pond. This is the key point, it's all about your perception of yourself. So you don't have as nice a car as your neighbour? Congratulations, you have just made them feel better about themselves. Well done!

The secret to this is recognising that other people simply don't care, so you shouldn't either. Whatever status or perception of status you gain from buying expensive stuff wears off quickly – it's empty financial calories, and if someone really does care about what possessions you own, and that is all they are measuring you by, they're probably not people you want to be friends with anyway.

Social media is a big problem. When I was growing up there were only a few 'Joneses': our actual neighbours, my friends at school and so on. Today you can say hi to thousands of Joneses every day on Facebook, Instagram, Tik Tok and the like. It's much easier than it has ever been to get an inferiority complex about other peoples' supposedly perfect lives. It's particularly bad for young people where withdrawing from social media is next to impossible if you want to interact with your friends. When some

Instagram celebrity influencer shows off their posh Mykonos holiday, they are setting a standard. Someone watches this, replicates and shares their holiday on their Instagram. Now their friends also want to have a similar experience to 'keep up', which perpetuates the cycle.

Of course it's fine to want to do this, but even if you can afford it, step back when you are spending money and ask what your motivations actually are. If more people lived for the actual experience and the present moment, and less for the social media moment, I'm pretty sure the world would be a better place.

I really don't care what other people think about me now. I just do my own thing and mostly buy what I want; if someone else has better stuff, good for them.[14] It's liberating. I certainly wasn't this way when I was growing up. When I was in grade eight (the year before secondary school in Canada), I remember going school shopping before I started at my new high school.[15] I went to the local K-Mart and bought some new supplies. I was becoming interested in basketball and wanted some high-top trainers. I saw some white vinyl Traxx basketball trainers for $12. I loved them and my mom bought them for me. I remember going to the local beach that evening with the family wearing my shiny new white vinyl Traxx high-tops. I was beaming. A week later I started high school. I was moving from a different school system so only knew five other students starting in grade nine out of the class of 100. I was also the shortest person, male or female, in grade nine which didn't help my situation. Within days, some older guys decided to pick on me and quickly made fun of my Traxx trainers. I didn't say much and just sucked it up, but when I came home, I hated those shoes. It was all about how I thought other people perceived me, not about how I perceived myself. Anyway, I soon changed my trainers, so it

---

[14] Except when my co-founder Paul gets better gadgets and tools than me. I don't like that one little bit.
[15] In Canada and the United States, secondary schools are called high schools and generally go from grade 9 until grade 12.

is a complicated anecdote – I'm not suggesting someone needs to become a social outcast in order to save some money, I'm just saying think about it. Cost and quality aren't always very correlated and often people don't need the top-quality choice. This is especially true when it comes to luxury retail. High-end fashion brands may be of very high quality, but really, the price never remotely reflects the actual cost of the items anymore. You are paying mostly for the brand name and its artificial scarcity.

Despite my bold claim that I don't care what other people think, I really do like having the coolest gadgets. But what I do is I set a gadget standard relative to my world. I'm talking relatively minor things like phones, watches, computers, wireless headphones and so on. I have a business peer and friend who also loves his gadgets. When he gets a new sports watch, I want the same one, if not better. When he gets new wireless ear buds, I want the same or better. Now if I don't get the item, as I often can't keep up with his budget, I'm just fine. It's almost a hobby, I know exactly what it is going to cost me per year, and I can afford it. But the competitive instinct is still there, and it's that instinct I need to recognise and manage. I take my hat off to anyone who can resist 100% of this competitive pressure, given how powerful marketing and social influences are – I can't, but I can see the spending urge for what it is and I can fight it before it ever gets out of hand.

I also recognise that, to a degree, I am competitive on behalf of my children. My children certainly have more than I did from a material perspective, and I'm sure part of this is because I'm living vicariously through them. I'm trying to give them things I always wanted but couldn't have and wanting them to feel good about themselves relative to their peers.

My first job in 1998 after graduating paid me C$45,000 a year in Ottawa. One year later I received an offer for almost three times as much from a startup in Boston. My disposable income skyrocketed. Besides selling my 1989 Toyota Celica GT[16] and buying a brand-new Volkswagen Golf GTI,

---

[16] I absolutely loved that car.

Figure 3.2 It's Not the Answer

I bought a game system. Actually, I bought four game systems, all at once, shown in Figure 3.2. I bought a Sega Dreamcast, a Nintendo GameCube, a Microsoft Xbox and a PlayStation 2. Why did I buy so many game systems? Because growing up, I was never allowed to own a game system. I desperately wanted a Nintendo, but my parents couldn't afford it. Did I then play video games non-stop? No, I probably played one hour's worth of video games in total. I didn't really love playing video games, I preferred going out surfing or cycling, but I loved technology, and I think I simply loved the idea of having them. Of course, when I subsequently saw them sitting unused in my room it actually made me feel a bit foolish, and did I get some massive gain in happiness because I had a GTI rather than a Celica – I did not. I wish now that I had just put the money aside for something I really wanted, it would have been so much more fulfilling in the long term.

My eight-year-old daughter happens to be a fabulous runner. I believe she'll run on an international level one day.[17] I was an excellent cross-country runner at a similar age, so I see a lot of similarities, but the big difference is that my parents were almost completely oblivious to my athletic pursuits. In my daughter's case she loves her running so I actively encourage it: I investigate athletics clubs and events; we do runs and

---

[17] Bear in mind that I'm obviously a biased dad.

train together. I'm mindful not to be pushy, but I'm consciously trying to guide her. However, did my daughter *really* need carbon-soled Nike VaporFlys? Of course not. Did she know anything about the performance characteristics of carbon-soled shoes? Of course not.[18] But now she expects them – I've created a monster. I pushed a fancy gadget-tastic shoe on my poor innocent daughter because it's something I care about. Every parent must deal with the dilemma of how much we guide and influence our children versus how much we let them figure it out. I'm highly conscious of this. But one area we probably do not pay nearly enough attention to is education about social pressures to spend.

Think about the motives for why you and your family are spending money, and pause for a moment if it's really about status and keeping up with the Joneses rather than actual need.

OVERCOMING SHYNESS WHEN IT COMES TO MONEY

Shyness can cost people tens of thousands of pounds over their lifetime.

Are you the type of person who chats to the checkout employee when buying groceries? Do you smile at people when you are walking down the street? Or are you the type of person who generally avoids eye contact and dislikes making small talk?

In general, the more comfortable a person is chatting to strangers, the more comfortable they probably are engaging with people on the subject of money. Many of the activities required to manage money well – negotiating, refinancing, getting repaid, sending goods back – require interactions with

---

[18] Does she know about carbon-soled shoes now? You bet.

10 THINGS I ~~HATE~~ LOVE ABOUT MONEY

other people so there is a real cost to shyness or social awkwardness when it comes to your finances.

This can manifest itself in many ways, but the most obvious one is asking for money back that is owed to you. Perhaps you went out with friends, and you covered all the drinks. Or you bought some supplies for your flat and your flatmates owe you. Maybe you are on holiday with friends and covered the car rental or paid for an extra tank of petrol. Worst of all you lent money to friends or family and they haven't paid you back.

I have a friend who I'll call Rolf.[19] He had a brother in-law who was notoriously short of work and was a struggling actor. He always had crazy money-making ideas and ventures, but he never seemed able to make anything work. One day, he approached Rolf with his newest idea that was going to help him finally get his life sorted. He determined that there were many roles for knights, and with the proper armour, he could audition in a spectacular fashion and win these roles. This way he would both kickstart his fledgling acting career and put some money in the bank. The only problem was, he couldn't afford the authentic costume armour. He needed to borrow three grand to invest in top-of-the-line costume armour; armour so good that movie sets would hire him both for his acting ability and his armour. Yes, it sounds absurd but Rolf, highly sceptical as he was, was curious how this would play out. Rolf lent him the full amount. Sure enough, the brother-in-law bought his armour and ... well, no one knows. The brother-in-law never mentioned the armour or the acting ever again to Rolf. And was Rolf paid back? Of course not. When I asked Rolf about this, he knew the brother-in-law didn't have the money to pay him back so thought there was no point in creating any family tension. But of course the tension is there until this day – it's a low level tension that sits unspoken between the two of them, and Rolf feels foolish every time he is reminded of the loan.[20]

---

[19] Name changed to protect the innocent.
[20] Which I do quite often. Because it is very funny.

You can't just change who you are, some people are simply more introverted than others, so how do you deal with the financial consequences of not enjoying conflict?

- If you are ever spending money in a group, set out the expectations in advance. It is always easier to deal with when you manage everyone's expectations clearly from the beginning and eliminate any potential areas of confusion.[21]
- If you are ever splitting a bill, do it straight away, don't ever say, let's do it later.
- Never lend money to friends or family. That is what banks are for. If you lend money, expect to never get it back, if you aren't comfortable with imagining a loan as a gift, don't make it.
- If you need to talk to a company about money, because you have been overcharged, or because you need to renegotiate or cancel a subscription and you are dreading it and feel really uncomfortable about it, don't just leave it, get a friend to do it for you. For some people, calling people up and complaining comes as naturally as breathing.

BEING A YES-PERSON

What about situations where you're not shy, but you often feel compelled to say yes. Do you have Nice Guy or Nice Gal syndrome? Lots of people simply agree to certain levels of spend because they don't like disappointing other people, or because the decision needs to be made instantly so there isn't really any time for proper introspection.

This is very common among parents[22] – toys, sweets, trainers, takeaways – people love their kids so it is really easy to say yes, especially if

---

[21] And use technology. I think a shameless plug for HyperJar here is perfectly appropriate.
[22] Probably most of them today. It certainly wasn't the case 50 years ago when I was growing up. My parents took great delight in turning down the most trivial requests for funding.

it is going to avoid a tantrum. I'm certainly not going to tell anyone how to parent, but it's definitely worth asking the question: would I have bought this if I hadn't been asked? If not, then maybe saying no more often might be worth it.

The same logic applies to adult friends and family. This is less about being shy or avoiding confrontation, and more about not giving into your desire to make other people feel happy. This behaviour often extends to people where there is no relationship at all: people who always choose the upgrade or give into a salesperson's suggestions. If you feel awkward saying no, you will often end up saying yes under pressure.

It's less typical to request money directly from others as an adult, but often requests aren't explicit, there is just an expectation that someone pays, especially if one person is richer.[23] Obvious visible examples of this are professional athletes who have often come from a modest background. They become instant millionaires and there is always an expectation to take care of the people where they came from. There is nothing wrong with being generous and kind, but there are so many examples of people damaging their own financial futures. In this case people often forget that the earnings of a footballer, for example, although high are very short-lived compared to other professions (see Figure 3.3). I don't expect too many millionaire athletes to be reading this book[24] but this phenomenon happens to all kinds of people when they get a great job.

Be generous but be generous within your means. Try to prevent any exchange of your money happening because of pressure or guilt. Be deliberate and intentional and ensure you want to do it.

When it comes to your money, make yourself happy first. Then you can think about what you might want to do with others. Learn to say no!

---

[23] Or perceived to be. I know plenty of people who have far less money that people think they do. Myself for instance.
[24] If you know any, lend them your copy and say hi from me.

Figure 3.3 People Have Different Earning Profiles

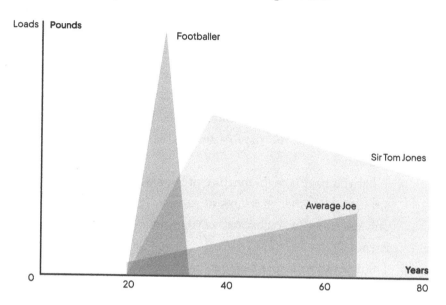

RULE 3 WRAP-UP

Money is not just about you alone, it's about your interactions out in the world. It's impossible to master your spending without considering your relationships with others, especially when it comes to money. If you can identify the people and companies which impact your spending, you will be well on your way towards reaching spending Zen.

Here are some things to keep in mind:

1. Almost no company you interact with is your friend. This doesn't make them bad per se, but their primary objective is to take your money. Always keep this at the front of your mind and disappoint them as much as possible.
2. Avoid lending or extending credit to people you know at almost all costs, unless you are prepared to never see it again. Nine times out

of ten you won't get it back. This is as relevant for splitting a bill in a restaurant as it is for lending someone money for a suit of armour.

3. Don't feel pressure to spend money just because others are doing it. You aren't a scrooge, or a miser. If someone is putting pressure on you to match their spending, it's because it helps with their self-validation and makes them feel better. It's not about you.
4. Try saying no to family occasionally when they are asking for ridiculous stuff. Trust me, the first time is the worst, then it gets easier and easier.
5. What you have is not a measure of your worth. At all. Ever. There are plenty of other measures of success. If you think someone is only interested in you because of your money then find some better friends.[25]
6. Think about your spending personality type. If dealing with others isn't easy, you will need to set out ground rules ahead of time. This may include avoiding situations where you may feel pressure or spend less time with people who cause you to get into trouble or do things you later regret.

---

[25] In my journey through life I've come across a lot of very wealthy people. In almost all cases the very richest are the least obvious about it. I guess they feel they have nothing to prove.

CHAPTER FOUR

RULE 4: THE SMALL THINGS MATTER

Don't overcomplicate this. We know spending is important, but do we know how important the small things are? They are probably the most important thing so let's understand and master this.

'We are what we repeatedly do. Excellence, then, is not an act but a habit.'
—*Aristotle*

'I spent a lot of money on booze, birds, and fast cars. The rest I just squandered.'

—*George Best*

10 THINGS I ~~HATE~~ LOVE ABOUT MONEY

What I hate – I hate how experts overcomplicate money which creates anxiety for so many people. There is way too much noise in the world of personal finance.

What I love – I love how money and spending follows the Pareto Principle, 80% of the benefit comes from 20% of the action. It's easy to get good with money, and small things make a really big difference over time.

How many retired professional athletes do you know who now look like they've never got off their couch? The truth is it's nearly impossible to maintain a world class level of fitness – which these athletes were required to do day in day out – and it's not remotely surprising that when one stops doing something hard, one tends to stop all together.[1] Interestingly many people who never take exercise to the extreme but simply live a good healthy lifestyle, maintain their fitness throughout their lives. Perfect equilibrium, where you spend exactly what you earn, never make any mistakes and regret nothing is nearly impossible to achieve, nor is it ideal. Just like the professional athlete, trying to be perfect at spending is exhausting and at some point you will just give up.

The thing about spending well is that it's about small easy changes. Because of this the results won't show up overnight. So how do you stay motivated? You need to remember one simple principle, and think about it all the time:

The compound effects of small changes really add up over time (for good or for ill).

Obviously, getting a grip on your spending has all kinds of benefits from day one – in terms of feeling in control – but never lose sight of the fact that spending well over time has a big payout. Hooray!

---

[1] Herschel Walker being a rare exception - a Heisman trophy winning American football running back who starred in college and the NFL. He subsequently became a member of the US Olympic bobsled team in 1992. He also ran track in college. He's still extremely fit to this day and fitness is a major part of his personality. A hero of mine.

What does this mean in practice? Another great health analogy: A recent study[2] looked at the diets of 1,500 children between the ages of 3 and 15. They then tested their cardiovascular fitness regularly. Teenagers who performed the worst ate roughly 226 more calories of ultra-processed food per day than the best performers. Similarly, the least fit three- to five-year-olds ate around 273 more calories of junk food per day.[3] To put that in perspective there are 260 calories in one solitary Mars bar. So, the equivalent of a single Mars bar per day was the difference between the most fit and the least fit. The key point is *per day*.

Let's take this Mars bar analogy a step further. To gain one pound of fat on your body, you need to consume roughly 3,500 calories more than you burn. Assuming you're at equilibrium with your diet and exercise and you then decide to leave everything the same except start eating one Mars bar every day. That would mean every 13.5 days you would gain a pound of fat. That means in one year of doing this innocuous habit,[4] you would have gained 27 pounds of fat. This might seem shocking, but to the person, the gain would come gradually and would be difficult to notice. But a photo taken at the start of the year and at the end of the year would yield far different results. Figure 4.1 shows the amount of fat (to scale) one would generate eating a Mars bar a day for a year. You might say eating a Mars bar

Figure 4.1   A Mars a Day

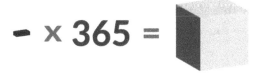

---
[2] Source: J.A. Vernarelli, E. Turchick and D. Melzer (2022) 'Setting the State for Childhood Fitness: Dietary Energy Density Is Associated with Locomotor Development in US Children', *International Journal of Health, Nutrition and Exercise Science*, 1(2).
[3] Source: Vernarelli et al. (2022).
[4] I do like a Mars bar, I have to say. Yum.

every day is absurd. But it doesn't need to be a Mars bar. It could be a bag of crisps or a sausage roll. The point is, it doesn't take much if you do it every day. But the good news is, this same principle works in reverse. So, if you created a 260-calorie deficit every day, over a year you would lose 27 pounds of fat. Now that's awesome.[5]

So the first big point here is that spending well, saving a little bit here and there, is just like not eating that delicious Mars bar. You don't have to do much for it to add up to really big amounts. I always love watching people on the TV show *Eat Well for Less*. The presenters say this revised shopping basket saves you £100 per week. The participants couldn't be less interested. Then they are told that this is over £5,000 a year and they are flabbergasted. Seriously. Multiplication – if you have forgotten how to do it, now might be the time to do a refresher course.

The really interesting thing about money saved is that it displays this multiplication effect on steroids: none other than famed scientist Albert Einstein remarked 'Compound interest is the eighth wonder of the world'.

Why is compound interest so powerful? Compound interest is basically getting paid interest on your interest. If you invest £10 at 10% interest per year, after one year you'd have £11. With compound interest, the next year you'd earn 10% on the full £11, meaning you'd earn £1.10. Then you'd have £12.10. And so on. This might not seem like much, but let's compare the returns on compound interest versus simple interest. If you put aside £10 per month for 30 years, you would have £3,600. Not bad. With compound interest at 10% this saving would be over £20,000. That's a lot of money considering you are only saving less than 30p a day. Figure 4.2 demonstrates the difference.

We'll talk more about compound interest, but now we'll talk about compound habits. Think of a compound action as something you do every day

---

[5] Yes, the Mars bar and the cube of fat are to scale. The fat-cube has sides of 23 cm. Drawing this made me feel slightly ill.

Figure 4.2 Awesome Compounding

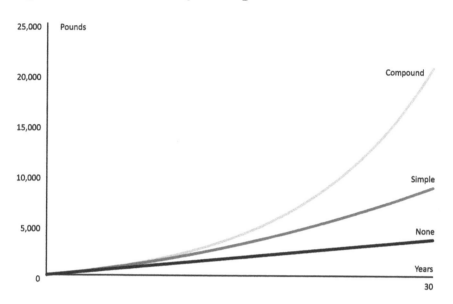

or regularly as opposed to once a year. Buying a posh coffee every day would be a compound action. After a year, you'd have spent almost £1,500 from this simple daily £4 purchase. If you rarely buy a coffee, it doesn't make much of a difference; but buy one every day, and it does. If you make lots of small purchases every day, next thing you know, any excess you had will be depleted.

How much does a small amount saved per day amount to over a long period of time? A great deal. How much does it amount to if you actually invest it? A very great deal indeed. The chart in Figure 4.3 shows how much saving a certain amount per day at a given rate over each of 1, 20 and 40 years. It really adds up.

That's right – saving £10 a day at a reasonable rate over a working life can leave you with a very large nest egg at retirement. Way more than the vast majority of the population currently saves over the course of their lives.

The tiny mistakes in behaviour that can affect your ability to take advantage of the benefits of compounding come in many shapes and sizes.

Figure 4.3 You are Kidding Me. That Much?

Years 1

Pounds per day

Annual Rate	1	2	3	4	5	6	7	8	9	10
0%	365	730	1,095	1,460	1,825	2,190	2,555	2,920	3,285	3,650
2%	369	737	1,106	1,475	1,843	2,212	2,580	2,949	3,318	3,686
4%	372	744	1,117	1,489	1,861	2,233	2,606	2,978	3,350	3,722
6%	376	752	1,127	1,503	1,879	2,255	2,631	3,007	3,382	3,758
8%	379	759	1,138	1,517	1,897	2,276	2,656	3,035	3,414	3,794

Years 20

Pounds per day

Annual Rate	1	2	3	4	5	6	7	8	9	10
0%	7,300	14,600	21,900	29,200	36,500	43,800	51,100	58,400	65,700	73,000
2%	8,957	17,913	26,870	35,827	44,783	53,740	62,697	71,654	80,610	89,567
4%	11,084	22,169	33,253	44,337	55,422	66,506	77,591	88,675	99,759	110,844
6%	13,825	27,649	41,474	55,298	69,123	82,947	96,772	110,596	124,421	138,245
8%	17,361	34,722	52,083	69,443	86,804	104,165	121,526	138,887	156,248	173,608

Years 40

Pounds per day

Annual Rate	1	2	3	4	5	6	7	8	9	10
0%	14,600	29,200	43,800	58,400	73,000	87,600	102,200	116,800	131,400	146,000
2%	22,266	44,532	66,798	89,063	111,329	133,595	155,861	178,127	200,393	222,659
4%	35,372	70,743	106,115	141,486	176,858	212,229	247,601	282,973	318,344	353,716
6%	58,162	116,323	174,485	232,647	290,808	348,970	407,132	465,293	523,455	581,617
8%	98,279	196,558	294,837	393,116	491,395	589,674	687,953	786,232	884,511	982,790

It really isn't about buying a car – the most common mistake is the innocent spend of small amounts that you simply ignore because, in and of themselves they're totally unimportant.[6] A spend that if you hadn't made it, the next day you wouldn't even remember the fact. How many of those spends do you do in a typical week?

Now add in bigger expenses, such as eating out for lunch, or paying for subscriptions that you don't use. If you're trying to save, the difference between packing a lunch and eating out could easily be £50 in a week, if not more.

---

[6] I define unimportant as anything you don't really want or need.

Rule 4: The Small Things Matter

For most people, finding material small savings isn't that hard; people don't because it all seems small, but it isn't. It's massive.

Pay attention to your daily habits. Pay attention to the small stuff. It has the most impact.

UNINTERESTING INTEREST

I'd like to take a quick look at actual bank interest and compare that to spending. Hopefully it can highlight how powerful smart daily spending decisions are relative to interest in a bank account. This is true even with the power of compound interest. I'm not discouraging you from investing your money in a savings account. In fact, I think investing is great (see Rule 10). The point of this is to get your spending house in order before you focus too much on interest. Right now with interest rates having finally got themselves off the floor, there has been a bit of an arms race in the banking world to offer higher interest rates on savings accounts.[7] However, for all the emphasis on the interest rate offers (and by the way, many of the headline numbers you see are teasers and come with lots of fine print), the impact this will have on your wealth is minimal if you have poor spending habits.

When we look at interest rates in October 2024, we see a range of rates across the market.

Default rates on current accounts at the major high street banks are quite low. Barclays has a free bank account that pays 0% on its current account. Santander Everyday current account is also 0%. NatWest Premier Select current account is 0%. Granted, these are current accounts but it's still your money sitting at the bank. Let's look at dedicated savings accounts. As of October 2024, the highest paying savings account in the United Kingdom is First Direct, Co-operative, HSBC and Skipton, all paying 7% per annum.

---

[7] Mainly from start-ups and challenger banks. Go take a look at Raisin, Flagstone and similar companies.

But oh wait, there's some small print.[8] The small print says that there is a maximum monthly deposit – £300 in the First Direct example – which would yield £136.50 over the full year if you fully maxed the account. Okay, so from 7% per annum to maximum annual interest of £136.50 no matter your balance. This is not genuine interest; this is an acquisition/marketing expense of the bank framed as interest. What it enables is the bank getting to the top of a comparison table which will lead to more eyeballs on the web.

Let's look at more standard rates without limits. If we look at that we see the highest interest rate on offer is 5.2% by Ulster Bank.[9] The average person still has their £1,000 in their current account earning whatever the bank offers them – even if someone moved all of their money to Ulster Bank, with all of the aggravation that that is going to cause, it's only going to generate £52 a year in interest. I'm not saying it's nothing, but compared to the amount of money a change in daily spending habits can generate, it's far less important. Unfortunately, the media likes to focus on interest rates (as do the banks) – too many people congratulate themselves on being smart with their money because they have switched bank accounts and stop right there, when a far bigger prize is right under their noses.

Let's go back to Figure 4.3 – let's *not* buy a coffee at Costa every day for £4. That's £393,000 after 40 years when earning 8% interest. It's quite incredible when you think about it. So when you cut out some of the small spends, don't think of it as a lost coffee, or a missing Mars bar. Think of it as going towards your small fleet of Ferraris.

We're going to talk more about compounding these smart spending moves, but don't fixate too much on interest rates. They matter, and it's good to keep banks honest, but it's a secondary concern. It's a concern and you should maximise it, but it's irrelevant if you're spending money like a drunken sailor.[10]

---

[8] They all have small print. Finance people like small print. I do. Hence all these footnotes.
[9] As of October 2024, *The Times* comparison table.
[10] Apologies to any drunken sailors reading this. I'm sure not all of you spend wildly, just using a figure of speech.

This is why I call it uninteresting interest. But fear not, once we are into surplus and accumulating savings, we're going to take all the uninteresting interest we can, and not fatten bank profits any further. But we're going to do this after we've put our spending house in order.

A LIFETIME OF MISTAKES (OR GOOD HABITS) ADD UP

Let's dive deeper into how daily habits compound just like money. This compounding is either going to hurt you or help you. Remember, if you are borrowing money to pay for stuff, the interest rate is going against you – lots of small amounts of debt over a long time can become a mountain.

People forget how quicky things add up. We have talked about calories and saving. How about running – a 500 m run each day? That is 183 km in a year. Or two hours of TV and social media each day? After a decade, you'll have burned 304 days – that's almost an entire year wasted.[11]

Mastering the small things is the most important thing you can do to improve your finances and become happier with money. I'll also make the point again that this applies for people who are rich or poor. The small things for wealthy people can lead to wealth destruction. The small things might be defined differently, but it's simply about daily habits that compound.

Imagine a mythical state of equilibrium, where your income and expenditure perfectly match. You are neither borrowing nor are you saving money (like eating exactly the right number of calories, Mars bars or not). If you recall from earlier in the book, for most people this is something

---

[11] Unless you were watching David Attenborough programmes, in which case you have just become frightfully educated.

around £50 a day. Now move this 10%, or £5 either way. Not much of shift is it? Over a lifetime the difference is one between being horrifically in debt versus having a very comfortable retirement.

I can't stress this enough – you have to put yourself on the right side of the equilibrium line. You need to understand your daily habits and stop the ones that are hurting you in the long term without you necessarily realising this.

There are exercises in later chapters to figure this out in depth, but I want to talk about one idea right now – somewhat of a controversial one – the Rule of Zero.

The Rule of Zero is simply this: for a period of time, stop all small discretionary spending (I call these 'straw-spends') without exception.

What's a straw-spend? These are the spends that equate to the proverbial 'straw' that broke the camel's back. These are the small inconsequential spends that you wouldn't miss a week from now, but that happen on a regular basis and eat away at your bank account and therefore become consequential over time. This is the coffee break, the snack on the way home, the trinket on Amazon. Getting the extra item in the 3-for-2 sale that you don't need.

More specifically, this means you cannot allow exceptions or breaks in whatever you are trying to change. It is the financial equivalent of going cold turkey for someone who is trying to quit smoking. Because of this analogy, it's somewhat controversial.[12] However, smoking and straw-spending are different – one is about deep dopamine cravings; spending can be addictive, but I believe straw-spending is more about awareness (or the lack of it). Once you become aware of the small actions, and understand the benefit of stopping them, or indeed the cost of enjoying them, it's much easier to stay on the path to financial enlightenment.

---

[12] After all, going cold turkey with substances has a very low success rate. Dr J. Taylor Hays of the Mayo Clinic had conducted research over a 25-year time span showing that out of 100 people trying to quit smoking cold turkey, only 3 to 5 succeeded for longer than 6 months (J. Taylor Hays [2014] 'Helping Smokers Quit in the "Real World"', *Mayo Clinic Proceedings*, 89[10], 1328-30; https://www.mayoclinicproceedings.org/article/S0025-6196(14)00743-5/fulltext).

I'm reminded of another theory called the broken windows theory. This suggests that visible proof of crime or anti-social behaviour in an area will lead to more crime, especially serious crime. Therefore, to prevent serious crime, an effective strategy is to clean up the smallest evidence of crime, including graffiti and broken windows.

The Rule of Zero invokes the broken windows theory of spending. By stopping the small inconsequential spends, we become more aware of our spending in general and are therefore less likely to impulsively buy a custom pink Range Rover with 24" rims on credit. If you have the ability to indulge and stay on track and in surplus, this rule has less relevance for you. But if you are struggling, give this one a try.

YOU ARE A FUNCTION OF YOUR ENVIRONMENT

It's important to note that life doesn't happen in a vacuum. We discussed the social side of money in Rule 3, how important being aware of your money relationships with friends and family are. Straw-spends can often happen because of the environment you're in so it's important to be aware of this possibility. The most obvious example is eating and friends. If your workplace goes out for lunch or if you and your friends like to grab a morning coffee together, that's all fine, so long as you're conscious of it and it's part of your intended spend. You need to want to make these spends. It could be entertainment, that's fine. Again, as long as you understand the consequences of these spends. How do we know the consequence of a small spend? A quick rule of thumb is simply multiply a given daily spend by 365 and see what that number is. Seriously, this single exercise is often enough to make you change your mind about straw-spends.

10 THINGS I ~~HATE~~ LOVE ABOUT MONEY

THE DISPOSABLE ECONOMY

When is the last time you fixed something around the house that stopped working? Or what about at your office? To its credit, the mobile phone market has created a secondary market of repairing screens as they are so commonly damaged and it's far more affordable to repair than throw away. But aside from the main brands such as Apple, there is a much smaller repair trade. If we look at appliances, laptops, game systems, speakers, it's the same situation; most things are thrown out when they stop working. This is partly because many items are much more affordable today than decades ago. I remember when our family got our first VHS player. We had rented a player and videotapes from the local Blockbuster equivalent for years until we finally got a shiny new one for Christmas.[13] The reason why we waited so long was because of the expense of such a player relative to my parents' income. Today, the issue for many people is less about their ability to afford electronics and, ironically, it's harder to afford the basics like food, housing, heating and education.

The global economy has done a funny shift over the past few decades with the emergence of global trade that has made the production of many clothing and electronic items very affordable. But the basics like food, housing, heating and education have not enjoyed the same productivity gains as technology. Therefore, they are taking an ever-increasing share of people's income. It has become normal to dispose of things that don't work. But more nefarious, many brands and manufacturers have built-in strategies to make it harder to repair items and either force you to replace them or go to the dealer for expensive repair work. I mentioned cars, which is a perfect example. The computerisation of cars has made repairs more

---

[13] It was one of the highlights of my childhood. What does this say about me? Or indeed my childhood?

difficult and more expensive. It is an issue for car manufacturers if people hang onto their cars too long. Fortunately for them, even if a car is well made, people want the *new new thing* in cars almost as a fashion statement. But more people are hanging onto their cars longer, which creates issues for manufacturers. Environmental regulations help them out a bit – a council puts in place a tax on older, dirtier vehicles so you need a newer model to avoid the tax. If you look at appliances and technology, the construction has fewer screws and more glue. This means once something is manufactured, you effectively must destroy it to look inside.

This disposable concept extends to clothing. Jeans manufacturers like Levi's and Wrangler would famously show everything their jeans can handle through years and years of wear. Now, there are fashion brands that release new styles every couple of months, and you'll be lucky if the clothes last that long. Since the clothes are so cheap people don't think twice about tossing them, but life wasn't always like this. We have been conditioned to throw things out. Imagine if we didn't have this mindset. How much money would you save? It's likely something you haven't thought about but it's worth pausing for a moment to consider as it may surprise you how much you waste. But I come back to the same point, it really isn't your fault – you are a victim of a modern economy where even the way things are built is designed to empty your pockets of money.

SUBSCRIPTIONS MAKE THE WORLD GO ROUND

It feels like these days almost every business offers a subscription. You have the obvious widely adopted subscriptions such as Netflix, Prime, Spotify and Disney+. You have some traditional subscriptions like Sky TV, newspapers and magazines as well as the gym. You then have social media subscriptions for Snap and Telegram, for example. There are app subscriptions such as those for dating apps or gaming. Then you have shopping and loyalty subscriptions such as for Ocado delivery or extra rewards from Sports Direct. Software you used to buy can often now only be available by subscription. I'm thinking about Microsoft Office but also think about most apps. Freemium is an app business model where you can get a barebones free version and then upgrade for a monthly or annual fee to the full featured premium version. This could be for storage such as Dropbox or notes tools such as Evernote or most fitness apps. Most apps now have this recurring payment model, and very few let you just pay once to own the software, the way they used to in the past.

Also, many smaller businesses offer some form of subscription. It can be for a product, such as Holos kombucha[14] every month. My veterinarian even offered me a subscription plan to help me save on vaccinations and any unforeseen checkups I might need for my dog.

The point I am making is subscriptions are now everywhere. Why do so many businesses offer subscriptions? Multiple reasons – for software and apps, it might be that the apps need constant updating and development so older versions will go out of date and perhaps become non-functional. But really there are two main reasons:

- They can charge you more. For reasons we now all know £10 a month simply seems a lot less than a one-off charge of £200. But obviously after a couple of years you have paid more. It is our old friend multiplication again.
- People often stop using a service; sign up for one TV show but don't bother or forget to cancel. The entire gym industry pricing is based around a premise that the majority of people won't actually use their subscriptions very much.

With card-based payment for subscriptions, consumers have lost another element of control in being able to easily cancel any subscription

---

[14] This is tasty stuff if you haven't tried it before. And good for your gut.

Figure 4.4 Subscriptions Are Everywhere

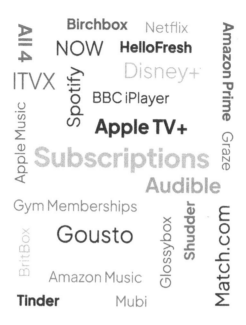

by stopping the payment. Now you must contact the company and ask them to please stop charging your card,[15] unlike direct debits and standing orders where the consumer can stop the payments. There are some card services now that will let you block payments from companies[16] but this is not common yet as it's a relatively difficult technical problem to solve. Figure 4.4 gives a sample of the many subscriptions you can now indulge in.

ADDICTIONS AND VICES

Sounds exciting in a finance book doesn't it? This is pretty obvious, but addictions are likely going to cost you money and hurt your mental health

---

[15] Not that easy for some people who don't like confrontation.
[16] HyperJar being one of them.

75

on top of all of the other potential harms. I'm sure if you have some really bad addictions you probably want to cut down or stop.

Sometimes it really helps to add up the cost of your addiction and compare it to what else you could have for the money. Use the table in Figure 4.3 to work it out. Sometimes working out the financial cost of a bad habit can provide the motivational nudge to help you to quit.

Take an honest look at your life habits – are any of these addictions? It could include things as innocent as clothes shopping. Once you have discovered any addictions, think about how you might try to curb these. Seek professional help if needed but don't ignore it. For people suffering here, fixing this will be life-changing and affirming.

EATING OUT WHEN YOU ARE ACTUALLY IN – FOOD DELIVERY SERVICES

It is so common now isn't it? From Deliveroo and Uber Eats to deluxe ready meals, convenience has never been more accessible. For a period of time, the food delivery services were getting in a fierce battle, adding more and more options and promising faster and faster service. I felt like I was reliving that scene from *There's Something About Mary* where the hitchhiker tells his brilliant idea to Ben Stiller's character. The hitchhiker describes a popular video called '8-minute abs'. So, his idea was '7-minute abs' – one minute faster, instant bestseller. Ben Stiller's character then suggested '6-minute abs' might be even better.[17]

So we have been in a similar arms-race with making food convenient. If we didn't want to do some sort of preparation at home, we used to have to go out, now it is so easy to spend without leaving the sofa.

---

[17] Personal recommendation. I loved this movie, some iconic hilarious scenes.

A food spend really is a big one, as it is one of the largest components of many people's budgets, and it involves choice, so it is one of the components which most people can do something about every day.[18]

When you start to rely on food delivery, then you have fewer groceries in the house, which makes it more difficult to make a meal; so in a way it becomes a reinforcing model.

The supermarket really is far more affordable, so if you rely heavily on food delivery, do the usual maths to understand the impact this has on your spending and have a think about how often you really need the convenience.

RULE 4 WRAP-UP

Small changes in daily spending will have a huge impact on your wealth and happiness. The good news is that these small changes can easily be made with a bit of effort.

- Small financial activity which is repeated has *big* consequences.
- Small actions lead to big consequences over time. This works both for you and against you. Good daily habits will help you. Bad daily habits will hurt you.
- By focusing on spending and eliminating waste, you can set yourself up for a much better financial future.
- Even a few pounds saved not spent adds up to huge things (saved not even invested).
- Interest on bank accounts is dwarfed by bad spending decisions. Focus your energy in the right place.

---

[18] Unlike your mortgage, utility bills and the like. Not that you shouldn't and can't optimise these as well.

- For some people, the Rule of Zero – a short sharp spending shock – is often required to understand how inconsequential 'straw-spends' actually matter.
- Managing the small spends also lowers the odds of making poor larger spending decisions as you will be more in tune with your spending in general.

CHAPTER FIVE

RULE 5: MASTER DEBT. THE GOOD, THE BAD AND THE UGLY

We're talking about debt which can send waves of fear into people. Let's confront this head on and take back control.

'Never spend your money before you have it.'

—*Thomas Jefferson*

'If you think nobody cares if you're alive, try missing a couple of car payments.'

—*Earl Wilson*

10 THINGS I ~~HATE~~ LOVE ABOUT MONEY

What I hate – How debt is too easily available and is often used by the most vulnerable.

What I love – How debt can be used to help you get wealthy if you know how to use it.

At any point in your life, you can decide to become healthier. And if you aren't living a healthy life, the best time to start is definitely today. There's little downside aside from having to make the effort, and I can assure you that becomes enjoyable if you're patient enough. There does come a tipping point where bad health and habits can creep up on you and create permanent problems. Even though the human body is incredibly resilient, if can only take so much.[1] So that is why today, you need to eliminate the health debt. And today, you need to come up with a plan to eliminate your financial debt.

SO WHAT IS DEBT?

Debt at its simplest is when someone owes someone else money. This simple concept has come to dominate global economies and finance. The total debt market is so massive that it is now three times the size of the global equity market.[2]

Debt is a big deal both in the business world and for individuals. In the business world there are lots of different words for debt – examples include: loans, fixed income, bonds, debentures, gilts, trade finance. In the consumer world there are even more products: loans, fixed income, overdrafts,

---

[1] Keith Richards aside, but I'm not advising you to copy his lifestyle.
[2] Global equity market refers to the value of all stocks that are traded on stock markets. For example, Apple, Microsoft, Google but also smaller public companies and those around the world (B. Tuckman and A. Serrat [2022] *Fixed Income Securities: Tools for Today's Markets*, John Wiley & Sons).

credit cards, mortgages, Buy Now Pay Later (BNPL), auto and student loans, hire purchase. Lots of names for the same thing which at the end of the day is someone owing someone else money and almost always with some sort of interest payment on top of it.

So let's talk about your debt.[3] You almost certainly owe some money to some company, probably a bank, but for the purposes of this chapter, it's you against the lender.

Lenders are really good at lending and making money from it and they are getting better and better as finance goes digital.

At first glance debt seems very complicated. But what I really want to get across in this chapter is that it's actually quite simple: there is basically good debt and bad debt. You should embrace the former and avoid the latter like the plague.

DEBT IN THE UNITED KINGDOM

The United Kingdom has the sixth largest economy on earth.[4] The UK GDP is £2.27 trillion as of 2023.[5] As shown in Figure 5.1, while the UK GDP was £2.27 trillion, the public sector debt was £2.69 trillion and private household debt £1.9 trillion.[6] That's a lot of debt that we're all contributing to – it's a national pastime.

When some countries that are financially challenged borrow, there are often onerous restrictions imposed on economic behaviour and spending

---

[3] If you don't have any well done. Have a gold star and go to the head of the class.
[4] Quite remarkable for a small island. It only trails behind the United States, China, Japan, Germany and India.
[5] Source: D. Clark (2024) *The UK Economy – Statistics and Facts*, Statista, July, https://www.statista.com/topics/6500/the-british-economy/
[6] Source: The Money Charity (2004) *The Money Statistics June 2024*, https://themoneycharity.org.uk/money-statistics/june-2024.

Figure 5.1 Mindbogglingly Big Numbers

Public Debt
£2.7T

GDP
£2.3T

Household Debt
£1.9T

by their lenders. I mention this because as an individual, when you borrow, there are also often restrictions and measures put in place, but these are usually only for certain kinds of debt like a mortgage you need to buy a specific house. But for a credit card or overdraft facility? You can pretty much do what you want. This can feel like freedom but also presents the opportunity for economic calamity if you're not careful.

A CLOSER LOOK AT PERSONAL DEBT IN THE UNITED KINGDOM

Personally, I find statistics around debt in the United Kingdom quite astonishing. My data come from The Money Charity (www.themoneycharity.org), which is a great organisation whose mission is to help everyone achieve financial well-being by managing their money well. These numbers (see Figure 5.2) fascinate and alarm me in equal measure. It makes sense when you remember we're a country of over 60 million people but it's still quite alarming.

Why do people use debt?

Figure 5.2   Mind Blowing: The Money Charity Statistics

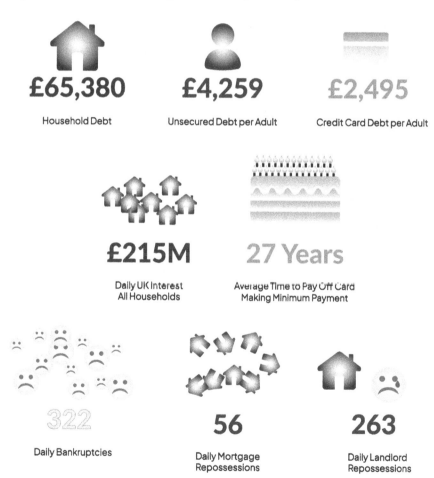

It might seem obvious at first glance as to why people use debt but let's dig deeper.

On the surface, there are many reasons individuals use debt. Let's start with the most common and work our way down:

- Mortgage to buy a house.
- Loan for a car.
- Loan to pay for university or other education tuition.
- Loans for home improvement.
- Credit card to manage cash flow and bills.
- Overdraft facility to manage cash flow and bills.
- Loans for purchasing larger personal items such as iPhones or computers.
- BNPL for purchasing clothes or shoes.
- Loans or leverage for investments.
- Financing holidays.
- Advancing your salary.
- Financing for almost any purchase you can think of.

When you look at this list do you see a natural division between two types of debt?

What is the debt actually doing? There aren't too many things debt achieves. It is attempting to do one of the following:

- Buy something expensive that you actually need but you cannot afford today (so rather than save up and buy, you buy now and pay down later).
- Smooth your cashflow (for example, cover expenses before the next payday).
- Mindless shopping.

I like to think about debt in simple terms, especially when trying to decide when debt might be helpful.

The first characterisation I use is debt for investment and the second characterisation is debt to buy things that depreciate or don't contribute to your future wealth. In the first instance, the debt can supercharge some smaller amount you have to invest in (that's why we call it *leverage*) and in the other instance the debt erodes your assets. This is because not only do you repay the principal, but you also have to repay the interest for something that eventually becomes worthless.[7]

The truth is, sometimes you just need to use debt to buy something that will depreciate but is necessary for life, but many people just use debt because they are impatient.

With this acknowledgement, we now have another way to reframe the previous list:

- Debt that is used to buy a house.
- Debt that you have to take out to cover necessities.
- Debt accrued because you are doing something for fun or pleasure.

What if we could combine these concepts and come up with a decision tree for when it's wise to use debt? I have done exactly this later in the chapter.

This reminds me of a painful story which I'm going to tell you. This story isn't about classic debt, but it is about using what we call leverage in financial markets. What I'm about to describe in this story is a way to invest (i.e. gamble) in financial markets on more shares than you have the money to actually buy.

About 15 years ago I was working for someone who hadn't paid me for about 2 years. It seems absurd to even write that down, but that's what happened. There was a sequence of events, some promises, a bit of 'wait until this deal closes'. I don't think it was malicious on their part as they were also in trouble, but it blind-sided me. I had savings so I could survive, but it

---

[7] Sometimes long before you have paid off the debt. Nasty.

wasn't comfortable. I was also expecting these promises to be kept. Around that time, my then wife was tired of renting and wanted to buy a house. I felt pressure.

At the time I had about £30,000 in an investment account. I was always a fan of Research in Motion, more popularly known as the manufacturer of the Blackberry. At this point in time, Blackberry was getting crushed by iPhone and Android. They had one last shot to try and compete, so they launched an entirely new phone with touchscreen operating system. It was called the Blackberry Z10. They had a lot of hype, and the phone user interface (UI) was well received. The biggest complaint was the lack of apps. I was a true believer, and for me it was an emotional and sentimental story because Blackberry was born from my alma mater and was close to my hometown. I bought Blackberry shares. The stock started to perform well, and my money doubled. I got cocky.

I decided to buy a bunch of out-of-the-money call options. These are financial derivatives that effectively let you buy a lot of potential equity for a lot less upfront cash. You do this by, effectively, borrowing. That is, the derivative could become worthless even if the underlying stock it's tied to has value. I loaded up on Blackberry call options. The next thing I knew, I looked like a genius. My options increased almost ten times in value. What started out at a value of £30,000 had grown to almost £300,000 in a matter of weeks. I hit some jackpot, but I wasn't done. I wanted £1 million to buy my house so I was going for it. I didn't cash out my winnings, I hung on, ready to reach that goal!

What happened in the end? Blackberry announced a disappointing quarter, the stock price dropped and my out-of-the-money call options cratered in value. My £300,000 of paper winnings fell to less than £3,000 before I finally cut my losses and sold. I lost it all. I learned many lessons with that. Pigs get slaughtered and don't let emotions rule investment. Don't gamble on markets as they are too volatile. Don't try and pick stocks. Don't concentrate your assets because it's too risky unless you're prepared

Rule 5: Master Debt. The Good, the Bad and the Ugly

to lose it all. Don't aim for a target with investments, and if you're using leverage and you've managed to win, get out. Painful, and to write about it now still hurts. The emotional swings to go from thinking you're an investing genius to the biggest moron within a day are quite humbling. (See Figure 5.3.)

The moral of the story? Don't ever borrow money to invest in anything other than a house.

Figure 5.3   Mat – the Stock Picking Superstar

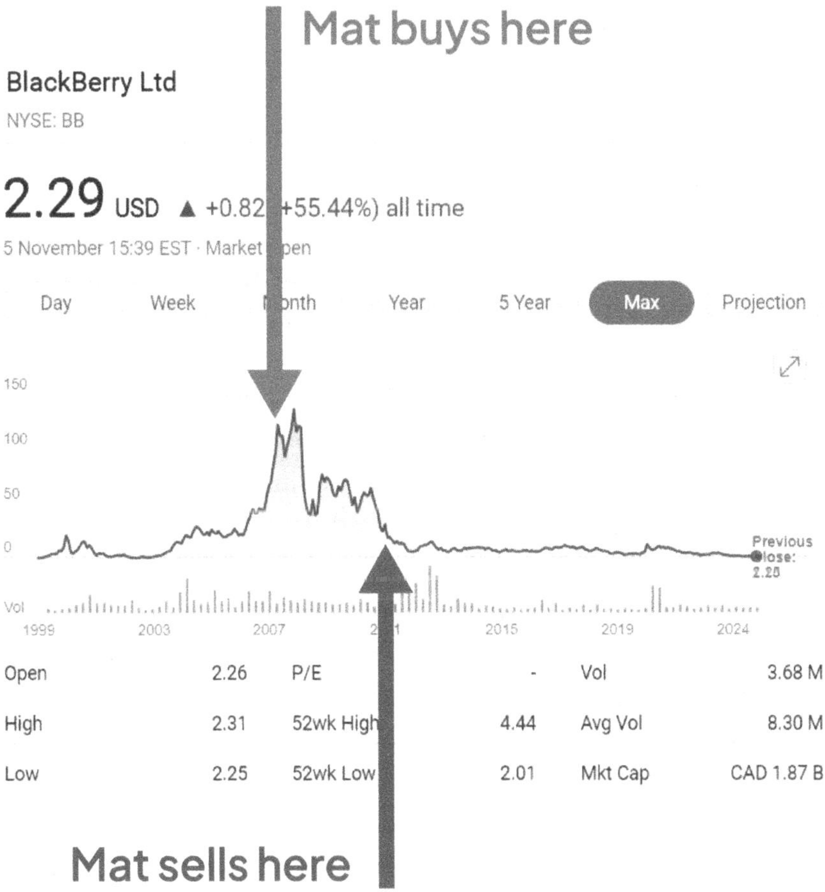

BlackBerry Ltd
NYSE: BB

2.29 USD ▲ +0.82 (+55.44%) all time
5 November 15:39 EST · Market Open

Mat buys here

Mat sells here

Open	2.26	P/E	-	Vol	3.68 M
High	2.31	52wk High	4.44	Avg Vol	8.30 M
Low	2.25	52wk Low	2.01	Mkt Cap	CAD 1.87 B

Let's now look at how debt can trap people. It's always good to understand how a trap works so if you're caught you can more easily escape.

DEBT TRAPS AND SPIRALS

This sounds ominous, but it's ominous for a reason. Due to human nature, and lender practices, once you get into debt it can be very difficult to get out unless you are very, very careful.

A debt trap usually starts with some sort of impulsive decision, or a real need. Those on higher incomes usually get into debt traps by chasing increasingly expensive lifestyles. Those on lower incomes usually get into debt traps either by spending on expensive financed items such as vacations or trying to pay for necessities that they can't otherwise cover, from car repairs and groceries to Christmas presents.

In all cases the debt load usually sneaks up on people and the sad reality is, more often than not, the first loans are taken out during a time of relative comfort and then grow over time, until it's too late.

The other complication is that interest rates are typically variable and can change over time. For an unusually long time, interest rates have been very low indeed. Recently, due to inflation, interest rates have risen. These rising interest rates have had a serious impact on any debt repayments by individuals, especially those having to renew their mortgages or anyone who is holding credit card debt. My opinion is that interest rates now are more normal and what we had experienced is unusual and unlikely to be repeated anytime soon. I would personally plan for interest rates a bit lower than today, but not too much lower.

Credit card debt is a classic debt trap. If you pay off your balance each month, you're fine. However, the credit card company provides some helpful guidance for making a minimum payment. I quoted this statistic earlier but on average, if a UK resident were to only pay the minimum amount on their credit card debt, it would take them over 27 years to pay off the debt entirely. That means in the end, you will have paid many multiples of interest compared to the original principal amount you borrowed. There are also predatory lenders who charge sky-high interest rates where the borrower ends up paying far more than the original value of the loan. It's this type of debt one should try to avoid at all costs. MoneySavingExpert gives a great example of how much paying the minimum amount will cost you. For £3,000 in credit card debt, paying the minimum over 28 years will cost the borrower £4,750 in interest charges, giving a grand total of £7,750 (see Figure 5.4). You can quickly understand how it would be difficult to get ahead and increase your savings if you're paying all that money away in interest.

Figure 5.4   A Life Time Occupation – Paying Off a Credit Card Debt

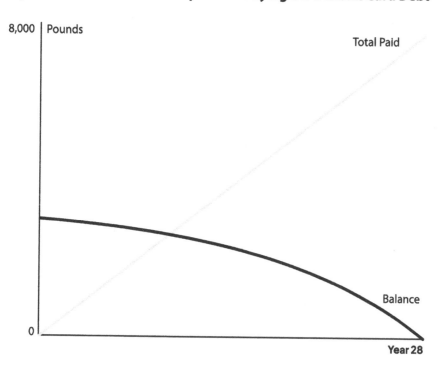

And this is assuming a reasonable normal rate of interest. Many cards and debt products have spectacularly high rates of interest.

How to Spot and Avoid a Debt Trap

Debt traps usually have, or are exacerbated by, the following:

- High interest rates. Sometimes mind-blowingly high. By law, all debt products have to provide their Annual Percentage Rate (APR). This is the effective interest rate taking into account all fees. Anything much over 20%, proceed with extreme caution.
- Low monthly payments, or payment holidays at the beginning.
- Easy or fast loan approval.

How to avoid a debt trap:

- Brainstorm all other options to avoid the debt, and especially if it's lifestyle choice debt.
- Have a proper plan for repaying the debt. Quickly.
- Never sign up to debt under duress or without advice.
- Avoid lenders who aren't monitored by regulatory agencies (here it's best to stick with a bank).

Once in a trap, here's how to get out:

- Rather than pay the minimum amount, try to pay the maximum amount.
- Look to lower your interest by consolidating debt or refinancing with a different lender.
- Consider personal bankruptcy if things are really bad (we'll talk about that more later as well as the best way to pay down debt – but it's a perfectly valid option that not enough people are aware of).

GOOD DEBT, BAD DEBT. WHAT'S THE DIFFERENCE?

What is good debt? What is bad debt?

I spoke about my classification earlier in this chapter and I concluded the following: We have a sliding scale for debt. On one side we have debt that is used for investment in both appreciating assets and life (for example, a car to get to and from work). On the other side we have spending related to depreciating assets and consumables. This could include necessary things like groceries.

The simplest definition I have for good debt is that it is anything that I believe will increase my DON, my Daily One Number.[8] I define and discuss this extensively later in Chapter 6, but for now let's call it my personal surplus. It can be a little complicated to calculate its impact because sometimes an investment may not increase your surplus immediately, or its second order, but I think in general you know. An example would be a car purchase for commuting to work. A car has a negative impact on finances due to car payments but has positive impacts: less time wasted so more time to work, reduction in other commuting costs and so on. Thinking about a debt-funded purchase like this is important though – attempt to quantify the benefit when looking at the cost the more affordable the car, the less negative impact it will have. These are the things we'll need to consider when determining if something is good debt or bad debt. To help us with this, I've labelled debt into three buckets: Obviously Good, Obviously Bad and It Depends.

---

[8] I'm introducing this here but there's a large section later in Chapter 6 discussing this. Your DON or Daily One Number is your daily money you have left over after accounting for all your necessary and committed expenses throughout the year. You take your annual income, subtract your annual expenses and then divide that by 365. If it's positive that means you are saving. If it's negative it means you're eroding your savings or are in debt, but you certainly aren't accumulating money. It makes you aware of how consequential small daily spends are to your overall life and will be the most important number to get you on track to a better future.

Obviously Good

Things that are obviously good can still be bad! A mortgage is obviously good because house prices typically go up, you need a place to live and it's better if payments are going towards owning an asset than paying rent to a landlord. A mortgage could be bad if you purchase a bad house, if you plan to move in a month or two, if it's for multiple properties and there's a housing slump, or if you bought way more house than you need, etc. But for the most part, for most people, a mortgage is an obviously good use of debt.

Obviously Bad

Debt that's obviously bad is pretty much always bad! I'm somewhat biased because I despise frivolous debt and have made a career out of trying to help people avoid going into any unnecessary debt. Take BNPL for example – this is debt used to buy stuff that depreciates in value that isn't necessary to live. Debt that is used to buy clothing, shoes, sports kit or technology is rarely the best thing to do. Pretty much 90% of the things people buy. Don't use debt to buy it. Save up to buy instead.

It Depends

This is the trickier stuff like debt used to manage real life cash flow crunches such as buying groceries, paying for an emergency car repair, or covering school expenses. It depends because you still want to avoid it, but sometimes you don't have a choice. But understanding why you don't have a choice is important so we can fix it and you'll never be in that situation again. Therefore, it's important to make this distinction.

Rule 5: Master Debt. The Good, the Bad and the Ugly

BANK DEBT DECISION CALCULATOR

We now know that debt is sometimes okay, often should be avoided and there's a bit of a grey area where things get more complicated. I've created a little decision tree to try and help you decide whether taking on a loan will make sense for you.

Before I do that, let's first look at how the industry today decides whether or not you can be approved for a loan. There are usually two big types of loans that a bank will consider, with different levels of risk. The most common is a mortgage for purchasing a house. The risk to the bank for this type of loan is less than a credit card because there is an asset (your home) that can be sold to help repay the loan (in a worse case situation of you defaulting). This is why the downpayment is very important to the banks, in case house prices do not rise, or to cover costs associated with foreclosing a home. The other type of loan is unsecured, meaning there is no asset to support the loan. The most common example of these loans are credit cards, BNPL and overdraft facilities. But people can also just get an unsecured loan from a bank for almost anything.

Let's first look at how a bank assesses mortgage affordability. They will perform a series of calculations but at its simplest, as shown in Figure 5.5, they look at:

1. Your credit report.
2. Your income.
3. Your expenses (paying special attention to required expenses such as child fees, insurance, loan repayments, regular utility bills).
4. Your job history (how likely is your income to maintain moving forward).

Figure 5.5   Lender Data

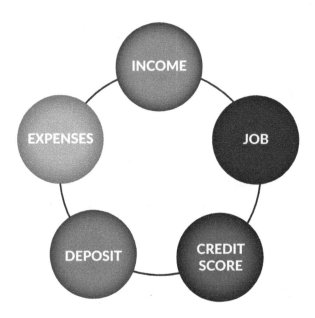

5. The size of downpayment you plan to commit.
6. Your savings . . . just kidding! Banks don't seem to care about your savings. I know because when I first moved to this country, even though I had significant savings, all that mattered was my income history in the United Kingdom. Thankfully times are changing and lenders are now including more datapoints to understand your situation better, especially newer non-bank lenders.

Using this information, they determine how much money you have left to afford, say, a mortgage based on today's interest rates and then they'll 'stress test' that result to see how you could handle payments if interest rates were to increase. There are subtle differences between banks, but for the most part a bank will give a mortgage equal to roughly 3–4 times your annual income. So, if your annual income is £50,000 a year, then you will be able to get a mortgage for roughly £150,000 to 200,000. I know this is crude, but it gives you a rough idea. The range is because they haven't yet accounted for your taxes and expenses and want to understand which expenses are absolutely necessary and which could stop if needed.

Now let's look at an unsecured loan, such as a credit card. This is much riskier for a bank, but also potentially much more lucrative as they can charge a higher interest rate. I did a super quick Google search on unsecured loans, and the first one that came up, which had a favourable 4.2 out of 5 stars rating, had an interest rate of 79.5%.[9] How someone does this and gets into a comfortable financial situation, I don't know. Let's not do this, at all, ever. I digress, I apologise for my rant.

You can tell right away that the dynamics with an unsecured loan are very different compared to a mortgage. There are no assets backing the loan so if you can't pay it back, they may have to try to extract blood from a stone.[10] The other very different dynamic is that the repayment almost always includes a much higher interest component. This is profit to the lender. Many of these unsecured lenders will recapture multiples of the original principal lent, yet still be able to put you into insolvency for not paying their interest fees. Why are the rates so high? They are so high because the lender is expecting lots of people not to be able to pay their loans back – so these defaults need to be subsidised by good borrowers. I just don't like anything about these types of loans.

So how is an unsecured loan affordability check conducted? Unsecured lending crudely looks at your free available cashflow and works out how big a loan you could repay. So, if you have £1,000 of free cash available each month, and you wanted a one-year loan, you could, crudely speaking, get a loan that works out to £12,000 in total including interest payments.

---

[9] OMG this is what we're trying to avoid people. Move heaven and earth to avoid EVER having to take out a loan charging 79.5%.
[10] It's unlikely to happen and they will have to enforce against you, ruin your credit score and ultimately take a loss.

Figure 5.6 Example Bank Lending Flow Chart

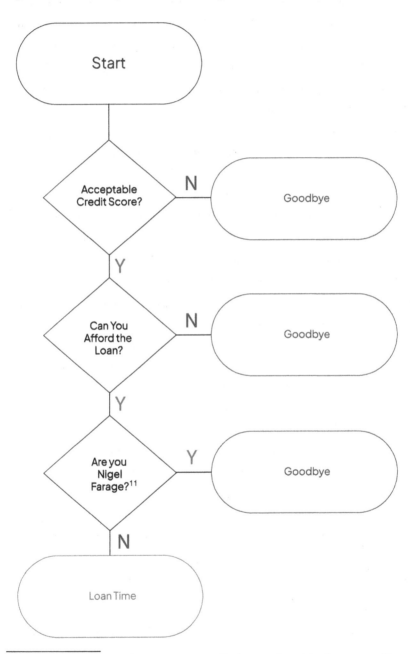

---

[11] This is referring to Coutts' decision to unexpectedly close Mr. Farage's bank account and in no way reflects any opinion on this matter!

Lenders look at how much money you have, and they will give you a loan that will take all that money. That's roughly it.

So, my cynical lender debt decision calculator goes like this, as shown in Figure 5.6:

1. What is your available monthly money after all your required expenses?
2. How long would you like a loan for?
3. We'll lend you an amount equal to how much money you have available to pay our loan off. You might be left with nothing after this, but as long as we're paid back, we're happy.

My point is that the lender's job isn't to look out for your well-being. Their job is to make loans and make a profit. It's an important service and it helps many people. But it also hurts many people. There is no guardian angel in the lending world looking out for your best interest. I'm your guardian angel now and we're going to do things differently.

MY DEBT DECISION CALCULATOR

Now let's get to my debt decision calculator (Figure 5.7). I don't care about how much you can afford to take out for a loan because I'm not trying to maximise the amount of debt you can handle; I'm trying to maximise your wealth.

My calculator will say yes if it's going to make you wealthier or drastically improve your quality of life. And when I consider quality of life, I consider the financial and mental load that debt places on a human.

I hope this decision tree has given you a sense of when it's appropriate to take out a loan. In my world, that will be anytime your net worth will go up as a result or when you literally have no choice.

Figure 5.7   Debt Calculator

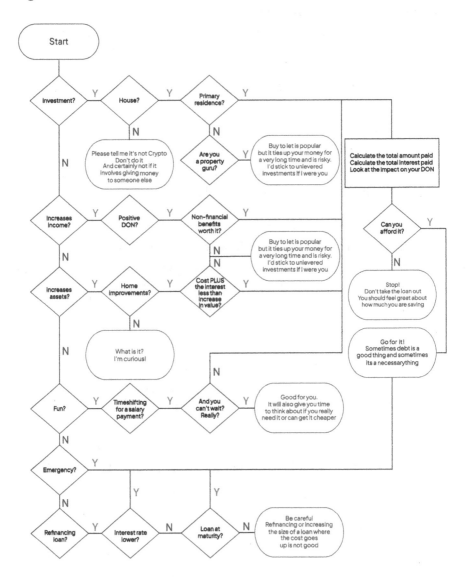

These calculations can be tricky as your short-term cash may take a hit when repaying the loan so it's best to get help if you need to understand if the loan will work for you in the long run across different life scenarios.

DAILY SURPLUS AND ASSETS AND LIABILITIES

To this point in the chapter, daily surplus (DON) was simply based on spending and cashflow for day-to-day expenses in living life. But when we start to accumulate assets and have liabilities that cost us, we really need to consider these as well.

How do we do this?

Let's look at assets – we'll start with a home. If you have a home, you likely have a mortgage. That mortgage is a liability or expense; however, that expense is paying off an asset. This is where DON becomes more complicated. All things being equal, would you rather have a rent expense of £3,000 each month or a mortgage expense of £3,000 each month? I realise there are lots of factors to keep in mind, but broadly speaking, most people would rightly say the mortgage payment is better. Why? Because it's paying for an asset. Rent on the other hand disappears forever once it's gone. But how do we account for this gain? Keep in mind you still gain if the house price never increases because you are paying for an asset that will have value in the future. Even if the house depreciates, the amount of depreciation is likely to be far less than the amount you have paid for rent. Interest payments make this calculation more interesting, but generally speaking, owning an asset such as a home is usually better than spending your money on rent. I say this as someone who has rented homes his entire life until the ripe age of fifty when I was almost forced into buying a house. This was not wise financial management for me but a factor of life circumstances and indecision.[12]

---

[12] I'm sure I have wasted millions. Learn a bit from me here.

STAY OUT OF DEBT

You hear me mention DON a lot and you're going to hear it a lot more later on when I properly introduce it, but that's because having a positive DON is the key to spending and financial freedom. When it comes to debt, the repayments are going to lower your DON and is not always the case that it is in any way mirrored or offset with a rise in income today. I'm trying to be nuanced because I understand there are times when debt really is required, but I also know people often tend to justify their situations and poor decision making and it's easy to convince yourself that debt you have taken on is good and necessary.

What I'm trying to really press you into asking yourself honestly, is this really necessary? If my life absolutely depended on it, and I had a clear frame of mind and some guidance, is there anything else I could do aside from taking on this debt? That's all I want to achieve here. And if you care and focus on your DON and look to grow that, you'll likely make the right decisions.[13]

LAST RESORT – PERSONAL INSOLVENCY AND IVA

This section is not very cheerful but it's important to discuss. All too often, people get mired so deeply in debt that they don't think they have any other options. Life can feel hopeless. I want to explain an option which is available to people when debt becomes unsustainable. In the United Kingdom, you have the ability to declare personal bankruptcy.

---

[13] Lots of people simply live at their credit limit for years. This is simply a full-time reduction in DON, often caused by purchases which have been long forgotten. I remember being a student too.

Bankruptcy is simply a way to deal with debts that cannot be paid. It involves entering a state of bankruptcy for a period of time and during that period a person's assets will be used to help pay off the debt. After some time, usually a year, outstanding debts will be written off. At that point, the person is discharged from bankruptcy. Someone can start this process themselves, or a creditor can initiate this process if a loan hasn't been paid back.

There are consequences to this decision and shouldn't be taken lightly, but for some, it's a genuinely viable option and should be considered. The biggest impact is a big reduction in credit score but is this so bad? Debt caused the problems so it's smart to avoid it again and start with a clean slate.[14] I'm amazed more people aren't aware of this option, or think that it isn't for them.

There are lots of things to consider, including eligibility, so if you feel this is something that might apply to you, I highly recommend you do some research. The National Debtline is a charity that has excellent information on the topic. They can be reached at www.nationaldebtline.org.

A less extreme option is an IVA, or Individual Voluntary Arrangement. This is a legal agreement between you and the lenders to pay back your debts over a period of time. The difference between an IVA and doing nothing is that the lenders should stop charging interest on your debts and also stop chasing you to pay your debts. Also, there are many types of debts which aren't eligible, including student loans, mortgages and money owed to HMRC. There are requirements you must follow when in this agreement and the costs can also be high – the charity Citizens Advice advises that you should not consider an IVA unless your debts are over £10,000 in total value. IVAs only work if you have a source of income to pay towards this monthly.

---

[14] It hurts most when it comes to home ownership, however. Getting a mortgage also becomes more difficult or impossible for a period of time.

RULE 5 WRAP-UP

This was a heavy section but with some concrete outputs.

1. Debt can be good, debt can be bad, and debt can be dangerous. The most important thing about debt is to never enter into any debt arrangement without deep thought and consideration. *Think about debt like you would marriage.*[15]
2. Debt that will increase your DON and wealth is good debt and should be seriously considered.
3. Debt that goes towards rapidly depreciating assets[16] is almost always bad.
4. Debt that is for emergencies sometimes cannot be avoided but try and think through all your options before you enter into it.
5. Debt is often presented as a short-term fix but then become a life-long burden. Be savvy when understanding how debt is helping you and how much it will cost.
6. If you are caught in a debt spiral and feel hopeless you have options such as personal bankruptcy.[17] Lenders aren't always interested in telling you this if you are still paying them.

---

[15] Not you Zsa Zsa Gabor, you need to think about debt differently. But everyone else, think about debt like you would marriage.
[16] Or assets you can eat or drink.
[17] There seems to be far more stigma about this in the United Kingdom than in other countries, for example the United States.

SECTION II

HOW

'Believe you can and you're halfway there.'
—Theodore Roosevelt

'Just do it.'
—Nike

The previous section looked at why spending and getting on top of finances can be so difficult. All of this involves introspection and getting clarity over us and our situation. This next section is more practical, providing specific steps on *how* to take charge of spending and finances.

CHAPTER SIX

RULE 6: AUDIT YOUR SPENDING HISTORY

It's time for your spending audit, which will reveal things to you that you were never aware of yet were happening right in front of your eyes.

'Nothing is as important as we think it is while we are thinking about it.'
—*Daniel Kahneman*

'Without data, you're just another person with an opinion.'
—*W. Edwards Deming*

What I hate – How financial statements and accounts don't make it easier to understand your financial situation. Open banking has promise but hasn't yet delivered.

What I love – Once you have understood where you have been its much easier to get to where you want to go.

Do you know your weight? Your height? Your blood pressure? Your resting heart rate? When you visit the doctor for a check-up, often the first thing they do is record some of these basic stats for you. Do you know how well you sleep at night, how much you can lift, how far you can run? The exact numbers aren't important, but an awareness of where you are physically is critical to knowing what you need to do next. The fact is that the people who are most aware of themselves are usually the people who need the least help. There's a reason for that. Awareness is almost a prerequisite to excellence. This is as true for money as it is for health. You need to understand the goals that will motivate you and stretch you, but not make you give up before you get started.

We're now aware of the importance of being mindful of our spending. We're also now aware why it's so hard to spend well in our modern digital economy. As we now understand what we've been dealing with, both consciously and subconsciously, it's time we understood our own spending to understand how close we are to mastery, or to misery. Don't worry if you are closer to misery. That means there's more upside and the exciting news is, the benefits will happen almost immediately.

HOW DO PEOPLE SPEND SO MUCH? LET'S ASK THE ONS

It's sometimes useful to understand how other people spend their money and to compare that to your own situation. Everyone has different needs and requirements, so this is mostly useful to have you possibly rethink some of your spending. It's very easy to become complacent and accept that whatever your situation is today is permanent. It's never permanent, life always changes but you can also make changes sooner if you have the inspiration to do so.

The Office of National Statistics (ONS) is a government office that collects data for the United Kingdom. They have tracked spending across ages, which is quite interesting. For example, it shows that for 18–55-year-olds, mortgage repayment is the largest expense. However, for 55+, the largest expense is recreation and culture. I doubt anything here is earth-shattering, but it gives you a sense of where money goes and how this shift will change as one gets older.

Figure 6.1 shows how the average UK household spend breaks down. How do you compare?

Figure 6.1 UK Household Spend Pie

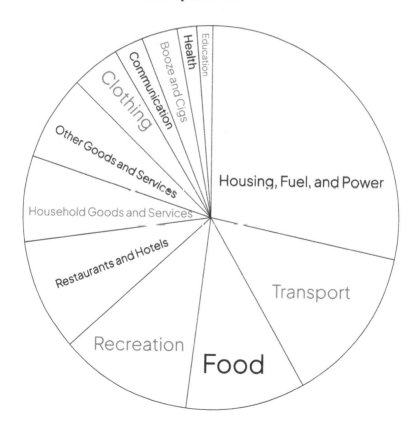

Next question – how much of this typical spend is really non-negotiable, and how much of it is amenable to a degree of discretion (see Figure 6.2)? Let's assume for a second that all of your essential spend is perfectly optimal.[1]

Figure 6.2 Discretionary Spend

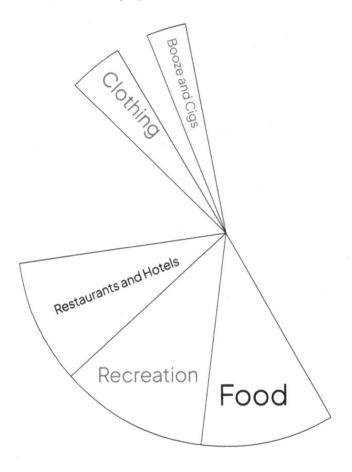

---

[1] Do me a favour. You can almost certainly renegotiate utility bills, refinance your mortgage and find a cheaper away to get around. But never mind.

This is not meant to be particularly scientific. I just want to demonstrate that a substantial percentage of most typical everyday spend is up for some degree of negotiation or management.

TIME TO GET TO WORK

For this rule you have to act.[2]

We're going to do several things.

- First, we're going to have a deep dive into your current spending.
- Second, we're going to pick out all the spending that we regret on some level.
- Third, we need to try and separate our solitary spend from our social spend and see if there are any patterns.
- Fourth, we're going to track all of our *spending under duress*. This is any spending you do that involves some form of pressure.

YOUR PAST. A SPENDING DEEP DIVE

This is the most important step in our audit. This is where we discover the biggest patterns and try to interrupt them. How we do this depends on what you use for your spending. This is one area where being digital helps immensely.

Before we dive into the banking app, let's first ask ourselves the following questions to ensure we are leaving no stones unturned:

1. How do I spend money? The options are typically with my debit card, my credit card, cash, online transfers and through friends or family that I pay back later.

---
[2] *Not* just read and nod your head in approval.

10 THINGS I ~~HATE~~ LOVE ABOUT MONEY

2. How many accounts do I spend money from? For most people, this will involve a credit card that is separate from your bank account. What's important here is not forgetting any accounts from which we actually spend money. I have to say, consolidating all of your spending in one place really makes doing this easier. I used to have lots of different cards for lots of different purposes. Result, not a clue what my financial position was, both in terms of positive and negative balances.
3. Do I ever have other people spend money on my behalf who I then pay back? This could be a friend who buys lunch for you or a colleague who is flying to Canada and you want them to bring you back some Coffee Crisp chocolate bars.[3] It's important we track this separately as our bank statements won't capture this level of detail.
4. How much seasonal activity do I have in my life and how regular is it? By seasonal activity, I mean regular patterns which will cause one month to have more spend than normal. Vacations, Christmas presents, annual membership renewals.
5. Lastly, let's account for all the anomaly spends. These are often random bad luck situations, such as getting a flat tyre, injuring yourself or helping a friend in distress. Think of these as rainy-day-fund expenses. Unexpected surprises that are usually unpleasant. It's useful to size this up to see how much extra we need to cover these emergencies.

Now let's start digging into our bank statements. If you are using a banking app without a web version, it might be a bit more difficult for detailed searches but that's okay. Can you use a spreadsheet? If you can then it's a useful tool for this, but scanning and taking notes will work just fine.

---

[3] Or Jersey Milk, or Mr. Big, or Crispy Crunch, or most controversially Big Turk (of which many friends have threatened to disown me over my love of this bastardized version of Turkish Delight. Mmmm delicious). Google these incredible chocolate (candy) bars and then try them, I implore you!

If you are using regular online banking, it's best if you can print off your statements to allow you to mark up the document. If you don't have a printer that's okay, we can still do this.

Step 1 – Download Two Years' Worth of Bank Statements

Ideally, we want to look at the last two years of spending.[4] One month of spend is still extremely useful. If we can get 12 months that is fabulous as we will capture big annual expenses such as car insurance, if you pay annually. The rule of thumb here is the more statements you can look at the better.

Step 2 – Scan Your Most Recent Statement and Start Taking Notes

Now that we have the statements, we're going to take a closer look. Let's start by scanning your most recent monthly statement. The spend here will be fresh in your mind and will likely be indicative of previous months. That is, this statement will tell you a lot about your spending habits.

As you scan, there are several things I want you to look out for. As you read through my list, I hope it inspires some other questions relevant to your life that only you know. You'll get a sense of what I'm talking about as you start making notes.

As far as making notes is concerned, it's best if you can make notes in a spreadsheet like Excel because then we can play with numbers. However, a sheet of paper or digital notes is also fine. The most important thing is we

---

[4] Well ideal would be all time, but we would rapidly be entering the land of diminishing returns. That said, if you are one of those people who like to do this then go for it.

need to summarise information to make sense of it and the bigger picture really helps here.

Step 3 – Questions to Ask Yourself

For each question, I want you to tally the total over the month.

1. How much of my spend is less than £5. How about £10?
2. How much of my spend is on eating out?
3. How much of my spend is at the supermarket? (For this one, I want you to think about how efficient your supermarket spend is – how much you waste and how much you regret. Just think about this for now as this comes a bit later when we optimise our spend. The important thing here is identifying patterns. If you spend £80 one week and £120 the next, we need to understand why there are discrepancies).
4. How much spend is greater than £100, £500 or £1,000?
5. What is your most frequent vendor you spend at and how much each month?
6. Are there any spends you don't recognise? How many?
7. How much spending was towards alcohol, cigarettes, vaping or gambling?
8. How much spending on coffee or tea away from home?
9. How much spend on group social activities?
10. How much spend was for emergencies or unexpected events like a car repair?
11. How much spending is for subscriptions? Here includes anything that is discretionary such as Netflix, Prime, Spotify, Sky, and premium apps like Tinder or Xbox Live.
12. Are there any subscriptions you don't recognise?

Rule 6: Audit Your Spending History

13. How many of your payments recur each month? This would be for subscriptions and utilities. Any of these you don't recognise?
14. How much of your spend is related to convenience, such as ready meals or grocery delivery and takeaway? Is your laziness costing you money?

These questions should inspire more thoughts regarding your personal situation. Browse your statements and compare to see if you can notice any interesting patterns. Looking for patterns comes naturally for some and can be difficult for others. That's okay. I'm going to list some patterns that you can try to look for.

Step 4 – Search for Patterns

1. Is daily spending similar? If not, what are the anomalies?
2. Do the same check for weekly spending and monthly spending. Is there seasonality to your spending? An example of seasonality would be spending increasing every December around Christmas or a typical example is the start of every month when all your bills are paid.
3. Do you tend to spend more in the evening or at lunch time? That might indicate online shopping habits.
4. Does your balance always tend to trend down to zero each month? Or to some other fixed number? This could be a good sign or bad sign, depending on the situation. It's good if you're sticking to a thoughtful budget but bad if you simply tend to spend whatever you have left each month and aren't saving.
5. Is your spending on holiday disciplined? Are you eating and doing thoughtful activities or blindly shopping for trinkets (either for yourself or the kids)?

6. Have your subscription and utility prices remained the same or have they increased? If they have increased, why? End of an offer period? The annual inflation-increase that many companies tend to do even when mid-contract?[5]

Hopefully these suggestions give you a sense of what to look for. We're just trying to see any changes, anything that seems odd, anything that surprises you which may be normal, but you just never realised it.

The simple act of looking over your bank statement, while potentially fear-inducing, is extremely helpful to ensuring we have the knowledge to make the changes we need to make.

BENCHMARK YOURSELF

Aside from the nuts and bolts of how other people are spending money that relates to us, how do you know where you are without context of where other people are?

How do you know if your spending is appropriate or excessive? Is the amount you spend on groceries reasonable? If you found out that someone very similar to you spent half as much each month on groceries, you'd be intrigued as to how they did it.

This is difficult to do as it can be very personal, but I'd recommend openly talking to close friends and family about your expenses and then compare them. Try to find someone as similar to you as possible. Ask about the utility bills, fuel, Christmas presents, groceries. All of this information is so helpful to inspire you to possibly change things. I'm working on a tool that will help people do this, but until that is built, you'll have to do it the old-fashioned way.

---

[5] I'll have a proper rant about this later.

THE PRESENT

How on earth can you possibly get your act together if you don't know what you have, what you have spent, and what you need to spend in the future? We've done an audit of the past and that also looks at the present.

We should have a sense of how much we need to live. But a sense is still a bit tricky, and we want something more concrete. What we're going to do now is do a few of the steps in devising something very close to a budget, but we're not actually going to make a budget. This doesn't preclude you from running a hard budget. That's up to you to decide but it's not necessary.

Present Audit – A Budget (But Let's Not Call It That. Let's Call It a Roadmap)

A Roadmap is a guide to how much we can spend each month.

Step 1 – Pick a Timeframe for Our Calculations

Monthly is the typical timeframe but we're going to dive deeper.

We're going to do this exercise over four timeframes:

1. Daily
2. Weekly
3. Monthly
4. Annually

Daily is extremely helpful because it puts a spotlight on your little daily habits that might be hurting you.[6] Weekly is useful as there are recurring spends that often happen weekly such as supermarket shops. Monthly is

---

[6] See Rule 4 for a reminder.

the obvious and typical timeframe as that is usually the cadence of how people are paid. Annually is important because this will capture big one off spends like auto insurance, AA memberships, vehicle servicing and annual subscriptions.[7]

Step 2 – Calculate Our Surplus or Deficit Using Monthly Summary Data

Let's do a quick sanity check first. Grab your past 12 bank statements, and we'll look at the monthly totals for money in and money out. We'll add up the totals for the year and then do our daily, weekly and monthly calculations.

For example, if someone earns £60,000 per annum after taxes, each month we will see money in of £5,000.

Then for each month we look at the money out. In this imaginary example, each month the spend is around £4,500 ± £500. So, each month the expenses range from £4,000 to £5,000.

The annual spend equates to £56,000. We simply added up 12 months' worth of spend.

Therefore, we have for income:

Annual income: £60,000

Monthly income: £5,000

Weekly income: £1,153

Daily income: £164

And for spending we have:

Annual spend: £56,000

Monthly spend: £4,666

---

[7] You'll notice the large number of automotive related annual expenses. I did this intentionally. Cars can be big money pits and it's important to understand how much income this takes from us to ensure we aren't wasting. I love cars so it's not just about practicality, but we need to be equipped with knowledge to not get ripped off.

Weekly spend: £1,076

Daily spend: £153

Now if we do the simple maths to get our net position – that is, our surplus or deficit – we have the following:

Annual surplus: £4,000

Monthly surplus: £333

Weekly surplus: £77

Daily surplus: £10.95

For those of you not in regular employment and drawing down savings, I want you to do a few simple calculations.

1. List the savings you'll be drawing down from.
2. Come up with the time period, in months, that you expect to have to draw down from these savings.
3. Divide the total savings by the number of months you need to rely on this. For example, if you have £10,000 of savings and need it to last you for 12 months, you will simply calculate £10,000 / 12 = £833.33 a month. This is our proxy income for purposes of a budget.

Be sure to capture all income, not just salary. For example, if you collect benefits or have income from property or other investments.

This hypothetical example has a daily surplus of £10.95 which equates to £4,000 over a year. Now I hope you're starting to realise how impactful small daily spending decisions can be in your life! How hard would it be to not have a Starbucks coffee every day and to not spend £5 on Amazon? It's very easy. We'll get into this more later on, but I'm hoping the power of my message is starting to really resonate.

Let's break down our surplus even further to an hourly number of £0.45 and a minute number of £0.0076 (or a fraction of a single pence).

I know this is ridiculous but at the same time, I find it fascinating how numbers can quickly add up. Each hour this person is saving £0.45. The point being, how easy is it to spend £0.45 without much thought? Or how easy is it, on a day out at Thorpe Park, to spend £30 on food. That would be three days of surplus burned. This daily number provides great insight. It's a historic number that is often a severe wake up call. Let's dig into this further to see how we can use this to enforce powerful positive behaviour change.

YOUR FUTURE. YOUR DAILY ONE NUMBER: DON

The daily number discussed in the previous section, your surplus or deficit, is a historic calculation. I want to now introduce a forward-looking concept to help guide your spending; it's what I call your Daily One Number, or DON.[8] This was briefly mentioned in Rule 5 so hopefully you are roughly familiar with the concept. I want to really explain it now, however. I'm going to use this expression a lot and it's probably the most important number you can focus on. The goal is to increase our DON and if it's in deficit, turn it to surplus. But if we only focus on one thing, if we have one north star that we use to guide our daily decisions, it's your DON.

Making better daily decisions involves a change of mindset and the benefits compound. This reminds me of a story my co-founder Paul told me. He used to smoke cigarettes. But one day he watched a video by British

---

[8] When I was doing my undergrad, I had a classmate and roommate called Don. Don grew up in Wingham, a small town in Southwestern Ontario and a sports rival of my high school in nearby Mitchell. We had a friendly rivalry at university, but Don always claimed he was a faster sprinter than me. One evening just before we graduated, at a party, me and Don finally had a race. And Don won. It was short, 30 m or so and I was catching up, but the point is I lost and until this day I feel ashamed. So perhaps DON is in honour of Don, who I think I would obliterate if we were to sprint today.

author Allen Carr[9] whose specialty was smoking cessation. Allen had said something that stuck with Paul and helped him to quit smoking. Allen said that the cravings one experiences as a smoker are the withdrawal symptoms of the previous cigarette. He concluded that the relief smokers experience when lighting a cigarette is not a high, but rather a feeling of being 'back to normal', which is a feeling experienced by non-smokers all the time. He then asserted that withdrawal symptoms are caused by fear and doubt in the smoker's mind and therefore quitting will be easy once you can remove any feelings of fear or doubt (Wikipedia). Paul listened to this and made a mental switch on the spot. He began to think of his cravings for a cigarette as his body healing. He began to enjoy them, knowing when he had this feeling his body was getting back to normal and that it would recover soon. He successfully quit.

There are many similarities to changing your spending in this day and age. Lots of spending we do is habitual but lots of it is therapeutic and driven by fear. Fear of missing out on a deal, fear of being bored. When you start to change your mindset and enjoy the thrill of accumulating money, the little changes we propose become easier and a part of your life.

How do we calculate DON? I designed this to be simple and intuitive. You can tweak this as you please – the important guiding point is to make you aware of your daily float and to be conscious of small and larger spends. Sometimes we get lost in the daily noise and forget the impact of our spending. DON will help you to avoid this.

DON is very simple to calculate. It's the historic spending exercise but we're going to exclude some things, namely non-recurring discretionary spend. This is very specific so read carefully.

DON = Daily income after tax – Daily necessary expenses

---

[9] Allen Carr the author is not Alan Carr the comedian. Even though I'm Canadian, I heard of Alan Carr (although don't know his material well) and that's immediately who sprung to mind when Paul told me this anecdote. I thought Alan Carr is quite the versatile professional. Alas, it was only upon writing this book that I learned this was in fact a different Allen Carr.

10 THINGS I ~~HATE~~ LOVE ABOUT MONEY

What are necessary expenses? These are all your direct debits, standing orders and repeat card payments. They include things which aren't really necessary, such as Netflix, but that you have committed to. So, this would be:

1. Rent/mortgage
2. All household bills such as gas, electricity, water and broadband
3. Mobile phone
4. Any streaming or app subscriptions such as Netflix, Disney+, Spotify, Xbox Gamepass
5. Gym memberships
6. Kid sports payments
7. All insurance including car/home/life
8. Groceries
9. Commuting and life travel expenses (such as fuel and rail tickets)
10. Anything else necessary to live your life

These are things that are part of our daily life, and we have made commitments for. We're not going to necessarily accept all of this moving forward, but we include them for now.

What do we not include? Almost anything else including:

1. Eating out for dinners or lunch
2. Coffee/snacks
3. Amazon/eBay/online shopping
4. Clothes/shoes
5. Vacation spending
6. Nights out
7. Donations to charity
8. Sports or movie tickets (any entertainment)

Basically, anything that is discretionary we exclude. I call clothes discretionary because we already have clothes, and I want to be ruthless when we decide to buy new clothes. So, I'm being a bit unfair, especially to parents.

This number becomes something we will be aware of every day. It will be what we have to budget with for our daily treats, our clothing, our longer-term holidays and Christmas gifts as well as our saving and investment aspirations. It will hopefully help us give our smaller spending decisions more importance when we realise how much of an impact they can have.

What's important to understand is once we have our DON, we're going to scrutinise how we can increase it. The easiest way to do this is not by growing your income, but by cutting your expenses. Some things are obvious, like Netflix, and some things might be trickier, like commuting expenses and utilities. But we'll scrutinise it all in Rule 8 and once you know your DON, you'll amaze yourself at how savvy you become at making it grow.

We're going to calculate this very similarly to our past calculations. There are a few simple steps:

1. We already know our daily income from the present calculation so keep that.
2. For necessary expenses start by going to your bank account statement and finding all the direct debits and standing orders you have set up. This will be neatly summarised and easy to add up. Double check the frequency. Most will be monthly, but some might be annual (if so, divide by 12).
3. Next, we need to locate all the recurring card payments such as Netflix, Spotify and any Apple or Android apps. You'll have to scan through your statement to find these, but you only need to do it for one month.
4. Lastly, find all our non-automated required expenses. This is usually supermarket spend, fuel and rail tickets/TFL. Add these up for what you think is a typical month. You don't need to do this for all 12 months unless you know your spend was extremely volatile.
5. Add all these numbers up to get your monthly 'necessary expenses' total. Next, multiple this by 12 for your annual total. Lastly, divide this by 365 for your daily necessary expenses.

6. Now that we have done this, DON is straightforward since DON = Daily income after tax − Daily necessary expenses

BRING IT TOGETHER: INCLUDE ADDITIONAL ACCOUNTS

As I have mentioned before, I should add that it's important we don't ignore other accounts that we may have. Most people have a main bank with possibly a current account and savings account. But it's also very common to have a credit card with another provider, a mortgage with a different bank, a savings account with someone else and a second bank account or spending card for day-to-day spend. If any of this applies to you, you simply need to ensure this information is captured in your DON.

Most of these accounts should ultimately feed back to your main current account by payments out to clear balances. If you have a credit card, you'll make a payment to the credit card from your current account. However, which categories your aggregate spending covers won't be known until we dig into the credit card statement.

With multiple accounts, it becomes even harder to have an intuitive sense of our spending and assets. By doing this exercise and finding our DON, we can now build up to where we want to go.

DREAM BIG

Congratulations, you've probably done the hardest section of this book. The hardest in terms of actual work and the hardest mentally. It's not easy

Rule 6: Audit Your Spending History

to look back at something you might be ashamed or fearful of. To look at your spending can fill people with dread. It's also painful work trawling through multiple accounts, getting statements, digging into the numbers. Now that you've done it, you've lifted a huge weight off your shoulders. Now we can move forward, forget the past[10] understanding our present situation and thinking about the future.

We should do a few extra steps before we move on to ensure we don't waste all this hard work.

I'd like you to do the following:

1. Write down your DON. Capture the income and expense side.
2. Look at your expenses and highlight ones that either surprise you or you believe you could reduce or eliminate.
3. Think about what your goal is for savings. Think about a big number and think about a timeframe. For example, let's say you want £10,000 and you want it in three years. We can do a quick sanity check on that number and then adjust the goal to something we feel is realistic. In this example, £10,000 over three years gives us a daily requirement to save £9.13. Maybe this is realistic, maybe it isn't. If you know your DON, it's much easier to sanity check this. But let's start with any goal that involves moving to surplus and saving over time.
4. Later we'll talk about how we become more ambitious, because the bigger your goals, the bigger the possibilities. We just need to believe them and have a plan to get there.

In later rules we'll dig deeper into what we can do to increase our DON. For now, just have a sense of what that is and then when we get to the specific steps, we'll be in a much stronger position knowing what we want and how to get it.

---

[10] Not totally forget, but don't dwell.

THE REFLEX: MOVE FROM CONSCIOUS TO SUBCONSCIOUS

What good is knowing your DON if we then have to move the earth to achieve it? Just like Allen Carr's smoking cessation tips, we're going to do this in a way that involves baby steps that you can easily incorporate into your life. And we're going to need to break some bad habits and build some good ones in the process. If we do this right, you'll just wake up, do your thing, and your DON will grow, and you'll put that excess to work. That's the goal. And this doesn't matter if you're rich or poor. If you have lots of wealth and income already, we're going to increase your surplus so you can have even bigger dreams. Perhaps it's philanthropy or a yacht. The point is, we're going to eliminate waste and regret. Waste and regret cause anxiety and they don't discriminate. Rule 7 is where we work out what our bad habits are and how we build some new good habits.

RULE 6 WRAP-UP

Rule 6 was a heavy one with a lot of work on your part. Let's look at what we learned and what's coming next.

1. We need to find our DON, our Daily One Number. This is the difference between our daily income and our necessary daily spend. This lets us know if our life is in surplus or deficit and by how much. By understanding this number, we can understand how impactful smaller purchases can be to our wealth potential.
2. When we do our accounting for our life, we mustn't forget other accounts and must dig into the details. Credit cards, savings

accounts, contributions to pension funds. All these accounts help paint a complete picture
3. It's quite easy to determine our daily income, but breaking down expenses and spend is more difficult. Later we'll figure out how to lower our expenses but for now capture as much as you can, so you have an accurate view of your situation.

Rule 7 will next talk about how we can take specific actions with the goal of increasing our DON.

CHAPTER SEVEN

RULE 7: BUILD NEW HABITS THAT WORK FOR YOU

Break bad old habits, make good new habits, then automate them.

'The first and greatest victory is to conquer self.'

—*Plato*

'I'm on a 30-day diet. So far, I've lost 15 days.'

—*Anonymous*

What I hate – How easy it is to have bad spending habits but not realise it because they have been normalised through a constant barrage of marketing and media.

What I love – When you finally realise what your bad spending habits are, they are easy to break and replace with good ones.

Habits are very personal. The habits that I need in order to get in shape will be different from the ones you need. The same is true for money and it's especially true for spending. We're all different, earn different amounts, and live totally varied lives, which is why it is so hard to be prescriptive in the real world. However, good habits have universal themes even if the application is personal. Let's understand how to customise good habits for you.

WHAT ARE HABITS?

The *Cambridge Dictionary* defines 'Habit' as 'something that you do often and regularly, sometimes without knowing that you are doing it'.

Habits are actions that we do that become so normal to us that we stop thinking very much about them at all. Spending is like this. We build a life routine that becomes habitual, and we desensitise ourselves to it being unusual in any way. But just because we don't think our spending is odd, it doesn't mean we don't have any bad habits.

I always brush my teeth twice a day. It's a habit, I don't even think about it. I still have to tell my kids to brush their teeth because if I don't tell them, they'll 'forget'. Do they actually forget, or do they not like brushing their teeth? I honestly don't know the answer. I certainly take their excuses with a pinch of salt. I have to ask myself why are they constantly forgetting to brush their teeth? Do all of my apocalyptic warnings of 'you'll get a cavity' fall on deaf ears? Why is that? I'm sure that the main reason for their apathy is that my kids don't really understand the consequences of having a cavity. Would they love having a needle in their mouth for an anaesthetic? Are they thrilled about the thought of getting drilled and having a filling for the rest of their lives? I doubt it.[1]

There is an analogy with money here. The long-term consequences of spending well seem too far away, the short term is often dominated by the dopamine-induced pleasure of shopping. Once you understand the pain of the dentist's drill it's pretty easy to brush your teeth.

Once you understand how nice it is to be on top of your spending, and the long-term positive benefits, it's pretty easy to develop habits to keep random spending in check.

HOW LONG IT TAKES TO FORM A HABIT

It has been popularly reported that it takes 21 days to solidify a habit. Apparently this 21-day benchmark originated from a 1960 self-help book titled *Psycho-Cybernetics*. In it, plastic surgeon Maxwell Maltz observed that his patients took around 21 days to get used to their new appearance after surgery. There wasn't any formal experiment, yet that didn't stop the book from applying this 21-day benchmark to a wide range of life situations, such as someone changing their mind about their beliefs.[2] In 2009, a scientifically rigorous study was conducted to test this 21-day hypothesis. They found that habits would develop between 18 and 254 days with the average being 66 days. The activities they tested were simple things like eating a piece of fruit with lunch. The key factor that contributed to success was consistent

---

[1] Unless they are even stranger than I sometimes think they are.
[2] If it's that easy, I should declare my MSPI personality mappings as declared science and spread them all around the world. Just joking of course. But then again maybe I would get on the telly?

daily repetition. Further study showed that different tasks will take different timeframes to ingrain the habit. For example, handwashing took a few weeks whereas exercise took half a year. This is important for you because we'll be discussing habits to master your money and it's important to understand that everyone will be different and that you must be patient and consistent before you see results. All that said, the habits listed below are mostly easier and quicker than brushing your teeth for two minutes, so let's settle on trying them for at least a month to see if they stick.

Some Bad Spending Habits

Let's look at some bad spending habits.

If we look at our personality axes (from Rule 2), we had three categories and an extreme for each. To recap, we had **Understanding**, **Acceptance** and **Impulsiveness**. If we look at the extremes, we'd have someone who is clueless or informed, accepting or defiant, and lastly reckless or thoughtful. Just because you have a type doesn't necessarily mean that you are going to be a good or a bad spender, it just may make it easier to adopt the good habits that you need. So let's first look at some bad spending habits and activities:

- Grocery shopping while hungry and spending too much.
- Buying food items about to expire.[3]
- Eating out too often (especially if you have groceries at home).
- Always buying lunch rather than packing your own.
- Buying bottled water rather than using your own water bottle that you refill.
- Buying things just because they are on sale (I have a concept called 'cost per use', or CPU,[4] to see if something is giving you enough value in the long run).

---

[3] Unless you are getting them at a discount and are going to eat them quickly, in which case full marks.
[4] My ex-wife actually came up with this and I would laugh at the time, but it's good and it helped reassure me with regards to some of her more expensive purchases.

- Lending money to friends.
- Covering costs for friends and not asking to be paid back.
- Automatically renewing any insurance or utilities after the contract ends.
- Paying full price when shopping (not using discounts, rebates or cashback).
- Spending your entire salary each month.
- Buying the latest iPhone when it's released (or Samsung Galaxy Flip[5]).
- Buying enough Deliveroo sushi to feed eight people when your partner is away, and you are on your own for dinner.[6]
- Buying clothes or shoes you never wear.
- Buying the wrong-sized clothing but not bothering to return the items to the shops.
- Buying too many bikes[7] (or anything else that you rarely use).
- Forgetting to cancel trials for subscriptions.
- Keeping memberships or subscriptions for services you rarely use.
- Giving into salespeople (whether they are seeking charity donations or selling something else).
- Not having longer-term savings goals (this affects day-to-day spending).
- Making lots of unplanned small purchases throughout the month.
- Upgrading to the next best option when buying larger ticket items (holidays, cars, subscription services, home furnishing).
- Buying extended warranty packages.[8]
- Waiting too long to buy something you need and eventually buying it, destroying its utility.

---

[5] Again, this is for Paul.
[6] You might guess who did this. Yes, my co-founder Paul. He once ordered so much sushi for himself that the restaurant provided eight pairs of chopsticks with his order.
[7] I like bikes, okay? They say the perfect number of bikes to own is $N+1$, where N is the current number of bikes you have. There may be some truth to this – but for the purposes of this book it's a bad truth.
[8] Sometimes these make sense, but honestly rarely, especially with electronics that already come with warranties and depreciate rapidly.

- Wasting electricity or gas, especially in the winter.[9]
- Not checking your bills or invoices to ensure they're correct.
- Automatically pressing the preset tip option on payment terminals even when you were not given any service.[10]
- Using the default settings for fees when you use charity donation sites.
- Using credit cards for everyday purchases and not paying down the balances each month.

I think this list is beginning to cover most situations where you are likely to erode your savings and decrease your DON. Next, let's talk about good habits and activities.

Some Good Spending Habits

Good spending habits don't vary by person or personality, they're universal, just like fitness and health. Everyone should be active and drink water. Everyone should spend their money thoughtfully and not waste it. Since the bad list was so exhaustive and these are opposites, I'll only list a few to give you a sense:

- Grocery shopping from a prepared list.
- Checking food expiration to minimise waste.
- Treating eating out and takeaways as entertainment, not as a necessary part of life.
- Shopping around for your car insurance and any contracts before renewal.[11]

---

[9] This is indirect spend, consuming resources that you will have to pay for. This can be leaving lights on, keeping heat on when you leave the house, etc.

[10] This is extremely common in the United States and increasingly Canada. Places where you would normally never tip have an automatic 'tip' screen when you go to pay.

[11] This is a huge bugbear of mine which I will discuss more later – mid-contract price increases. A good deal can get decidedly worse if mid-contract price increases are part of their terms.

- Rarely paying the full price (MSRP) and ensuring you get discounts.[12]
- Not wasting money on labels. Quality sure, like an Arc'teryx jacket is well worth it.[13] Rather, try to avoid paying £80 for a Supreme t-shirt.[14]
- When you buy something that doesn't fit, you return it and get your money back, saving your receipts and original packaging just in case.
- Keeping track of your subscriptions, and especially free trials and ensuring you only keep subscriptions you use and value.
- Being confident telling people no.[15]
- Being disciplined when buying things and not always choosing the upgrade.[16]

THE FOUR PHASES OF SPENDING

I'm sure when you read the two lists above you nodded quite a few times and identified with some of the items, both good and bad.

The big question is, how do you stop doing stuff from the bad list, and do more stuff from the good list? And more importantly how do you turn them into habits to make them stick?

The lists above are quite long, and non-exhaustive. How can you remember all of the different things which you should be doing better? The answer is we don't need to remember such a detailed list – all of these positive actions come from the same underlying principles.

---

[12] This is where apps like HyperJar try to be useful by centralising deals and value in one place, so you don't have to spend too much time searching. Plug-ins like Honey on web browsers are also very useful.
[13] Massive Arc'teryx fan here, guilty as charged.
[14] Apologies to Supreme fan boys and girls, I don't understand you at all.
[15] I will discuss this more later but saying 'no' is one of the most important skills to have in life. How often have you regretted something because you said yes, often because you felt pressured or guilt?
[16] There is an entire science in marketing around choice selection which you need to be aware of and we'll discuss more later. But typically, there will be three choices, and one is deliberately bad and tries to steer you to a more expensive one (that per unit would be better value but likely for someone who doesn't need all the units).

Figure 7.1 The Four Phases of Spending

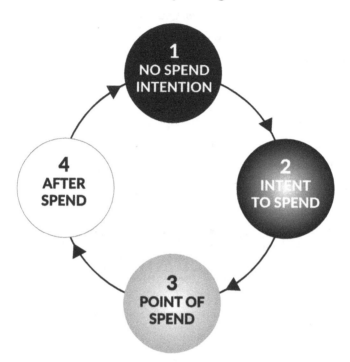

Let's start by setting out the spending journey in four distinct phases (Figure 7.1).

What I want to demonstrate is that there are a very small number of general habits (let's call them **meta-habits**) which, if you begin to adopt them, lead you to the path of spending zen quite naturally.

Phase 1: No Spend Intention

This is the base state, where you are not currently planning to spend any money, maybe you are having a bath?[17] It's a good place to be, in terms of

---

[17] Note: my ex-wife was quite capable of spending whilst in the bath.

keeping what is in your pocket, but you can't stay in this state forever since you need to buy stuff pretty much every day. All that said, if you have the odd spare moment, this is a great time to work on the first meta-habit:

Take some time to think about your spending on a regular basis.

Don't ignore it, don't just audit your spending once then walk away. Just look back over the last few days or a week, and:

- Check your balance (or balances) and what you spent over the last few days – you should do this regularly, if not every day.[18]
- Compare what you have spent with your DON (after a very short amount of time you won't even need to think about this, trust me).
- If you have been doing a good job and are creating a surplus, enjoy it. You have more money than you would otherwise have had, work out what it is. Marvel about what it is going to add up to over time. Save it.

That's it. Look at your spend and work out which historical spend is on the bad and good habit/activity list. It will make you so much better at managing the next few phases. Also make sure you know how much you have in total, and how much more you have because of your excellent spending behaviour.

Phase 2: Intent to Spend

This is where you start to think about buying something, but you haven't done it yet. This phase can be long (you are buying a house) or vanishingly short (an impulse online purchase).

So the second meta-habit:

Learn to pause a little more when you are planning to spend.

---

[18] Having a banking app which notifies you of your spend is great for this, otherwise you are waiting for monthly statements which is no good – you need to be able to see what you have spent whenever it takes your fancy.

The more Phase 2 is extended, the more good things happen.[19] You have the time to reflect on:

- If you actually want/need something at all.
- If you need it now, or if it might be cheaper in the future.
- If there are alternatives.
- If there are places where you can get it more cheaply.

You also increase the chance of avoiding spending which is driven by externalities like:

- Your mood: being bored, sad or tired increases the chance of bad spending.
- Your cravings: being hungry or a bit addicted or needing a dopamine rush – these cravings can pass.
- Marketing: have you just seen an ad or some product placement.[20]
- Other people: are you being steamrollered into some spend by a friend?

People who are Clueless, Accepting and/or Reckless often spend far too little (or no) time in Phase 2 when they are in a spending cycle.

Try to automate regular basic spending which you always do, so you don't have to spend too much time thinking about it.[21]

For non-regular spending, just slow down, breathe and work out if you need something right now or it can wait a little while, or a day or two. Even if you know you are going to buy something, just building in a general buffer is a great way to reinforce the second great meta-habit.

Do you know how one of the best spenders[22] I know manages Phase 2?

---

[19] Obviously it's possible to spend too much time in this phase, where you enter a form of paralysis and research something to the point of diminishing returns. Remember the 80/20 rule.
[20] And are clicking through straight to the point-of-spend without a single pause? God bless weblinks and cookies.
[21] But do not forget about it so much that you don't adjust it if necessary.
[22] Third dan black-belt Zen master spender.

- Unless it is unavoidable, or is completely regular spend, she simply notes down what she is thinking about buying in a list on a Post-it.
- She does all of her spending in one go on a Saturday morning.

Nothing else. This means:

- Lots of time and brain-space is saved during the week.
- There is time to percolate, either consciously or subconsciously about all potential spending.
- Opportunities for reckless mood-based spending are largely eliminated.
- It's very easy to see the total impact of spending on DON because the majority of discretionary spend is done in one go.
- The increased feelings of control and being on top of spending feels great.

Extending out Phase 2 by taking a little more time before you pull the trigger on spending is one of the best ways to avoid bad spending habits developing.

Phase 3: Point of Spend

Time to shop. Try to:

- Pause, if only for a second, and decide if you should really still be in Phase 2. There are lots of occasions where simply waiting 24 hours won't make a difference to anything at all. If this is the case, try it out occasionally – delayed gratification if you like.
- Spend the money. Congratulations. But, and this is the third meta-habit:

Shop around and spend as cheaply as possible.

There are all manner of simple ways to buy more cheaply than you think (see Rule 8). For all of my criticisms about how easy the digital world makes reckless spending, it also makes finding bargains and cheap prices extremely easy. Take advantage of this.

Phase 4: After-Spend Reflection

You have spent your money. It doesn't matter if it is seconds or days later, you need to: reflect on *specific* spending and decide:

- If it was good or bad, and how do you feel about it?
- Should you have spent longer in Phase 2, regardless of whether you feel happy about your spending?
- The point of spend is not always the end. If you don't like something you have purchased, or you aren't sure about a subscription, more often than not you can send an item back or cancel a service. You need to get good at doing this if you ever regret spend.
- If you have spent your money well, take a moment to pat yourself on the back.

So the fourth big meta-habit:

Spending isn't over until it's over. Reflect on each specific spend.

This will turn you into an expert spender. Everyone makes mistakes, especially spending mistakes. If you can build a healthy habit of reflection, you'll figure out how to make fewer mistakes in the future.[23] Having this mindset will be the most important tool to improvement.

---

[23] I highly recommend reading a book by Carol Dweck called *Mindset: How You Can Fulfill Your Potential*, which talks about feedback loops from reflecting on mistakes and how this will pay lifelong dividends. It's a great book (especially for parents trying to raise children who won't be traumatised by competition or pressure).

Rule 7: Build New Habits that Work for You

OTHER STUFF TO THINK ABOUT

All of the four mighty meta-habits above have a really big overarching theme – become more *aware* of your spending. I'd just like to touch on a couple of points which are really worth focusing on.

Be Aware of Your DON

By knowing your DON, and looking at what your recent spend is, you start to learn to appreciate what small (or large) purchases are costing you. This cuts across all four phases of spending. Many people don't give a single thought to a purchase after they have made it, it is just one more piece of digital debris in a bank account they rarely look at. It really takes no time to do a quick review. You need to start to look at each spend as:

- An absolute amount of money you now no longer have. You have actually given something away in exchange for a purchase.[24]
- A meaningful percentage of your DON. A £20 spend becomes much more mentally meaningful if you realise that it wipes out your remaining DON and pushes you out of equilibrium (or not).
- As something that you have purchased which, as an absolute fact, reduces your ability to purchase something else instead, and maybe something big, if you add up lots of small purchases, as we have seen earlier in the book.

By becoming more aware, you can start to make digital funny money feel a lot more physical and real. This is especially important for the small spends which are now so easy to ignore until you get your monthly

---

[24] The best things in life are free – but an awful lot of things aren't.

statement or credit card bill and find that you have spent hundreds of pounds.

Everyone can benefit from pausing and thinking before they spend money, but who are the MSPI types who need to work on this most?

- **CDR**: Ostrich – why on earth did I buy that?
- **IDR**: Addict – I've done it again – how am I going to stop doing this?
- **CAT**: Pleaser – why did I let them talk me into that?
- **CAR**: Nightmare – got to get a grip.

Be Aware of Marketing

When we become consciously aware of how often we're marketed to, we can start to learn to be tempted less. Our use of smartphones and social media means that most of us are being marketed to almost all of the time.

A useful exercise is counting the number of ads you see in a day. Literally keep track of every single one and then do a tally at the end of the day. I promise you that this simple exercise will yield a surprisingly large number that you won't forget in a hurry, and you'll then be mindful of the forces lined up against you.

Try to look at your spend and work out what stuff you bought because the manufacturer or seller marketed you. Are you really into brands?[25] Think about why.

This is most interesting to the following MSPI types:

- **CDT**: Hoarder – did I really need the 13th coat?
- **IAR**: Coveter – who was I trying to impress? Does owning this make me happy?
- **CAR**: Nightmare – Yes, me again.

---

[25] I always find it very strange how many of these supposedly rare and exclusive brands are on so many high streets, in so many airports, and are bought by so many people. If LMVH is so terribly exclusive, how do they make such staggering amounts of money? Expensive perfume, what on earth is that about?

Think About What You Have

Does this one feel a bit woo-woo?[26] I don't think it is. There is a lot of science behind the benefits of simply writing down a list of what you have and trying to feel good about it, and how much this can decrease stress and anxiety. Often when people shop, it's because they are bored, not because they actually need something else.

Start by taking a mental inventory of things you own that you like. It could be clothing, your smartphone, a book.[27] Think about why you like what you have got. Do you have some gaping holes in your personal inventory? Without seeing marketing or something in a shop, have you suddenly realised that your life is meaningless without another pair of socks? I'm not even talking about getting rid of stuff at this point.[28]

Next think about things you have and like that you don't use often (or at all). Think about why you bought this stuff. You either:

- Should never have bought it in the first place. A good lesson.
- You actually want it, but haven't got round to using it, or haven't used it recently. A great example of this is kids toys. My kids are always buying the next shiny thing when there is usually a huge inventory of fun stuff to do. It's the same with adults.

A focus on what you actually have can definitely have big ramifications in helping you understand what you actually need, spend less, and feel better for it.

---

[26] For those who aren't in the know, woo-woo is slang for something that feels mystical, supernatural or unscientific.
[27] This is a great one. If you have books and perhaps lots of books that you haven't read yet, you're not alone. There's a word for these people and it's called Tsundoku, aka acquiring reading materials but letting them pile up in one's home without reading them, according to the Cambridge Dictionary. I'm not referring to myself either ... ahem. But if this is you, take one of those books and start reading it. It will satiate some boredom, discourage you from adding another book to your collection and perhaps inspire you in some way.
[28] You should. And you should sell it on eBay. I'm a huge fan of simplifying your life and owning less – it's very liberating. Read Elaine St James and Marie Kondo.

This is most interesting to the following MSPI types:

- **CDT**: Hoarder – Don't I already have this?
- **IAR**: Coveter – How happy did I feel after the last time I bought something similar?
- **CAT**: Pleaser – Did I really buy all this stuff for myself?
- **CAR**: Nightmare – all of the above.

Create Friction in Your Spending

We have talked about trying to take more time over spending, but what if you need a little help? When I say 'create friction', what I mean is, making it a little bit harder to spend your money, rather than relying on willpower alone. This is a Goldilocks situation where too much friction is bad, but too little friction is also bad.[29] Some ideas:

- Don't keep all of your money in one place where it can be accessed directly by your credit card. Many modern bank accounts allow you to set up pots, vaults, envelopes, spaces and of course Jars,[30] where you can separate funds into many sub-accounts which can help you know in advance what you have set aside to spend. Even just getting a separate spending card and moving some money across once a month from your main account is a very popular way of setting some sort of circuit breaker on discretionary spend.
- Move surplus money up into a savings account, or even better an investment account (see Chapter 10). Out of sight, out of mind.
- Use cash for regular small real world spending (while it is still possible, it's getting harder and harder). You can see it, and you can't spend more than you have got out of the cashpoint.

---

[29] We have discussed how the lack of friction caused by digital payments makes spending so very easy. And there are countless firms trying to make it easier still.
[30] May I modestly suggest that the Jars in HyperJar are the best most functional version of this. Don't believe me? Try it out.

- Build a process for bigger spends where you always plan to have a quick chat with a friend or family member (hopefully someone who is a bit more sensible or frugal than you are[31]).

Friction works, if you get it just right.

Set a Few Clear Goals

This one doesn't require much explanation. This is often a great idea for all areas of your life, especially health and fitness. When it comes to finances, this is usually summed up in a single magic word, setting a **budget.**

I confess to being a little conflicted here – part of the whole thesis of this book is that by getting on top of a couple of very simple ideas surrounding day-to-day spending, everyone can get most of the way towards a much greater state of financial wellness.

Budgeting has always held a couple of big challenges for me:

- It takes a certain type of person to budget well, and frankly most people don't fit this personality type, so can't be bothered.
- The most common experience with budgeting, like setting out an ambitious exercise or dieting schedule, is that people overdo it in a burst of initial enthusiasm and so set themselves up to fail.
- Budgets are typically based around restraint and denial, *'I'm being careful with my money because I want to avoid bad things happening'* rather than focusing on the payout: *'if I spend well now, I get to do some really cool stuff in the future'.*

So I want to step away from the word budget and talk about setting a very small number of meaningful goals. Remember, whenever you set a goal, you become more conscious of factors that contribute to that goal and

---

[31] Not your YOLO pal (You Only Live Once).

thus more likely to achieve it. Even if a goal isn't reached, if it's a positive goal you will likely make positive steps in your life.

Some good short-term goals:

- Reach equilibrium with your spending.
- Increase the surplus from your DON after your spending.
- Make more good spending decisions. You can count them.
- Make fewer bad spending decisions. You can count them as well.

Longer-term goals are great, especially if they help you to feel excited about the future. Chapter 9 is all about changing the narrative about money and making managing it enjoyable, and having some good long-term goals is a part of this. Much of life is about anticipation, indeed the anticipation of a lot of achievements is almost as fun as achieving the actual goal itself.

Some examples of good long-term goals:

- Save up for a deposit on a house.
- Pay down debt or your mortgage.
- Get your retirement plans in order.
- Buy something utterly fabulous that you didn't think you could afford.

Calculate Cost Per Use (CPU) Before You Purchase Something

My ex-wife was a regular user of the CPU argument.[32] To be fair it was often a surprisingly compelling analysis, so I felt it is worth incorporating here as I've seen the benefits first-hand.

CPU is basically a relatively non-scientific way of determining if something you plan to buy is going to get used. CPU is simply defined as the cost

---

[32] Usually to justify the more expensive option.

divided by the number of times you will honestly use something before it breaks or before you throw it away.

A good example might be a baby pram. Imagine that there might be a model that costs £100 and a model that costs £500. Imagine the expensive pram will last 5 years and the cheap pram for 1 year. In this case both prams will have an identical CPU. But wait, is your child really going to be in the pram for 5 years?

Imagine a fancy handbag that costs £500. You can clearly buy a handbag for a lot less than £500 but is it going to be as nice or desirable? How does one justify this? Again, I'm not advocating using this to justify wasting money, but it's helpful to understand the longer-term impacts of larger purchases. If someone plans to use the handbag every day for 20 years because they love it, the CPU is going to be very low, if they are only going to get it out of the cupboard once a year, it's very high.

Of course, CPU really comes into play for bad purchases, not for justifying posh handbags. It is quite amazing how often I find that calculating a CPU purchase can make me think twice about buying something. A car in central London? What if the CPU is much higher than the cost of taking a taxi?

The cost of double glazing versus the difference in a heating bill. That posh handbag versus all of the things you could spend money on for every day you would use it.

Imagine Physical Cash at Point of Spend

Don't let yourself become desensitised to the value of money just because it's digital.

Try to visualise the physical coins and notes that would be needed to make a particular purchase as if you had them in your pocket. Then imagine them not being there. Ooof.

It is also useful to think about relative value, either on a fractional or a multiplicative basis:

- This spend (on a handbag) represents 20 trips to the cinema.
- If I don't keep doing this for five months (going to the cinema) I can buy that handbag.[33]

Check Stuff in Real Time

We have discussed one of the meta-habits in Phase 4. Reviewing stuff rapidly after you have completed a transaction. A great skill is learning to check bills in Phase 3, as you make purchases. People and places get bills wrong all the time. I feel like I'm in a minority when it comes to checking bills in restaurants, flicking through receipts in shops, checking if discounts or coupons have been deducted, making sure that tips haven't been added twice.

I know it's hard to make this into a habit if it's not something you currently do. Hopefully by reviewing your spending specifically (Phase 4) and generally (Phase 1) you will start to naturally want to do this – no one wants to feel like a mug when they check a bill the next day and find that they have been charged twice for something. Start by watching the register as your items are scanned and check your receipts. When you shop online, double check the final amount including shipping costs, never mindlessly click through the checkout basket.

I don't know why, but this habit can be hard because of some sort of social stigma, so it's hard for people who are Accepting rather than Defiant. People often don't want to:

---

[33] I'm sure you can guess my preference.

- appear to check a bill in front of friends or staff
- hold up the queue in a shop in order to question something.[34] To have to question something with a queue forming in that environment can be stressful.

Try to get over it. It doesn't matter – people really don't care.

Keeping Receipts and Packaging

Keep track of your receipts – I take photos of mine, it takes less than a second.

It's great if you ever want to remind yourself how much you have spent on stuff. Remember bank statements don't break down the individual line items on a bill[35] so they never give you complete information on spending.

There is another great reason to keep receipts, and also to keep packaging until you have decided you are absolutely sure you are going to keep something.[36] This is because you really can send stuff back. You really can. I can't believe how many people don't do this, even with quite expensive items. We have definitely developed a disposable culture.[37]

Try and make this a habit. Every time you buy something, ask yourself if you want to keep it and if you don't, return it. Know your warranties and use them.

---

[34] If you've ever shopped at Aldi, which I love, you will have experienced the fastest checkout staff in the country. Whoop!

[35] This is going to change over the coming years. It's going to be great. Watch HyperJar for details.

[36] For some expensive items I keep the packaging forever since it can help with resale. Lego Deathstars anyone?

[37] Research conducted by MyVoucherCodes showed that younger generations are in the habit of simply throwing out broken goods and buying replacements even if still covered by warranty. The conclusion was an estimated £423 million a year was being wasted on abandoned electrical goods. The survey further showed that a fifth of Brits never even checked warranty terms and a third have never made a claim on any faulty issue covered under a warranty. This was conducted over five years ago so I suspect the amounts would be even greater today ('Shoppers buying new household appliances rather than claiming on warranties are 'wasting £423 million a year'", *Mail Online*, 3 March 2018, https://www.dailymail.co.uk/news/article-5458937/Shoppers-buying-new-appliances-wasting-423million-year.html). Keep your receipts, unpackage carefully and use your warranties.

Keep Track of How Much You Waste

It's not just good for your wallet, it's good for the environment.[38] Not wasting stuff feels good for multiple reasons. Waste can come about in multiple ways. Let's list a few biggies:

- Food: Don't overbuy. I used to buy way too much and have to throw stuff in the bin. What was I thinking? It's very easy to buy less perishable stuff with minimal effort.
- Utilities: Get a smart meter. Switch stuff off.
- Streaming services: It may seem hard to do but don't be shy to cancel any subscription you're not using often. If in doubt cancel, because you can always resubscribe again.
- Memberships. This could be gym memberships, National Trust, play gyms, or leisure centres. Check your memberships and cancel those you don't actively use. Be especially careful of memberships that auto-renew. The best way to find these is usually reading your bank statements. Make sure during your spending audit you flag these and cancel them immediately.
- Perfectly good stuff you throw away: You would be amazed and flabbergasted by what you can actually sell. When you upgrade items, see if you can sell the earlier version.

Think about your life to see if there are any other areas where waste exists which you can eliminate.

---

[38] If you care personally or you are trying to impress someone.

RULE 7 WRAP-UP

There are four phases in the spending cycle:

- Phase 1 – No Spend Intention.
- Phase 2 – Pre-spend Intentions.
- Phase 3 – Point of Spend.
- Phase 4 – Post-spend reflection.

There are four meta-habits from which all other good habits flow:

- Take some time to think about your spending on a regular basis.
- Learn to pause a little more when you are planning to spend.
- Shop around and spend as cheaply as possible.
- Spending isn't over until it's over. Reflect on each specific spend.

CHAPTER EIGHT

RULE 8: SPEND LESS BY FINDING DEALS

Stop leaving money on the table and start stretching every pound.

'When it is obvious the goals cannot be reached, don't adjust the goals, adjust the action steps.'

—*Confucius*

'Shopping is a sport, and the clearance rack is my arena.'

—*Unknown*

What I hate – How most retailers don't actually reward loyal behaviour and instead try to take advantage of those who are complacent.
What I love – How easy it is to save money with minimal effort – if you aren't complacent.

A LITTLE LESS CONVERSATION, A LITTLE MORE ACTION

Every January, gyms are flooded with excited new customers determined to finally get in shape. It's wonderful to see but can be annoying for regular gym goers accustomed to a certain availability of equipment. Ahem. The thing is, regular gym users never stress too much, because they know, like clockwork, that the majority of new users will be gone by February. The problem is, you'll never get in shape if you only have a plan but don't actually execute it.

So, let's talk about Phase 3 – Actually spending your money. When it comes to spending well, knowing how to pay as little as possible for stuff is a critical skill, and you need to make it part of your general strategy going forward. The good news is that it's a lot easier than going to the gym, and it doesn't cost you any money, quite the reverse.

INEFFICIENT MARKET THEORY: DON'T BE AN EASY MARK

In finance there is a concept called the Efficient Market Hypothesis.[1] It broadly asserts that the price of stuff fairly reflects all available informa-

---
[1] If you are interested (for some mysterious reason) it's easy to look up on Wikipedia.

tion, which is why it's very difficult indeed to beat the stock market, since everyone knows what you know.

In the context of this book, my Retail Inefficient Market Hypothesis states quite the reverse, that the prices you see as a consumer are almost universally inflated from their true value.

Almost every retail business will list a price, the MSRP (Manufacturer's Suggested Retail Price) but then will offer discounts to this price. There are some rare exceptions, such as Apple and Porsche, but even these brands have discounts if you know how to look for them. Broadly speaking, most brands have their official price and then the price they're actually willing to sell at.

Let's look at the world of consumer products and services to help better understand why this is so.

Multiple Different Ways to Sell You a Product

Imagine a major brand, a product you are familiar with. This could be Apple, Coca-Cola, Nike, BMW or Colgate. Brands have three ways to sell their product:

1. Direct (online or physical).
2. Through distributors (such as John Lewis or Amazon).
3. A combination of 1 and 2.

Lululemon is a brand that sells direct. You can't buy Lululemon on Amazon or at John Lewis. Nike and Apple are brands that sell both direct and through distributors. Brands like Colgate and Coca-Cola will sell almost exclusively through distributors.[2]

To take an example:

- John Lewis buys television sets from Samsung at a price less than MSRP in order to be able to sell it to you for MSRP otherwise they

---

[2] I say almost exclusively because many brands now have online direct sales.

would make zero profit.[3] Same goes for Amazon for everything that you buy there. I'm going to estimate this distribution cost at roughly 10% order of magnitude.

- If Samsung were to sell the TV direct on its website, they would be able to earn the full margin on the sale. In fact, they would probably be delighted if you bought the TV for 5% less than MSRP because they would make a huge amount more than they would if you bought it for MSRP from a shop. Remember that you need to take out their cost of actually manufacturing the TV and all of the other costs before you work out their profit.
- Now of course they won't do this. If they actually put stuff on their website at less than MSRP they would massively compromise all of their distributors who do such a great job of selling their kit. It's already a problem for big bricks and mortar retailers where people come into actual shops to look at stuff and then go and buy it online.
- The key point here is that you aren't just paying for the TV, you are paying for the TV and for the distributors' profit margin.

What are the consequences of this?

- Brands are more or less flexible with their MSRP pricing policies. For many products you can often find that different distributors, or indeed the direct manufacturer, will sell you products at different prices based on their cost of distribution, their expectations of profit margin and their business strategy.

Let's take another example:

- Cars are almost exclusively sold through franchised dealerships.
- Tesla is an exception. They are pretty much the only manufacturer who sells cars direct in the United States and the United Kingdom.

---

[3] In fact they would make a horrific loss because they have to pay for stores and lovely staff.

Dealership associations have actually sued Tesla to try to force them to sell through dealerships. Each side claims potential savings to consumers depending on which side is doing the research. Wherever the truth is, it's undeniable that it is a change from what currently exists today.

The main point here is that the cost of what you buy is fundamentally linked to who you buy it from. Even where a manufacturer enforces a flat MSRP on all of its distributors, different channels can offer you all forms of incentives to buy something off them for full price:

- Vouchers and coupons.
- Money off on future purchases.
- Free stuff when you buy direct. Phones are a great example: special colours or engravings; free cases or earphones.
- Loyalty points or other freebies.

We've focused on products, but a lot of these concepts also apply to services. This includes sporting and theatre tickets, restaurants, as well as holidays, vacations and flights. Sometimes any discounts are embedded and harder to find but they are almost always there.

Retail Inefficient Market Hypothesis #1: The prices that you see from different channels are going to be different.

Why Merchants Never Expect Most People to Pay Full Price

So let's assume I am a manufacturer of a very expensive handbag,[4] which costs me £100 to actually make. This means that I can sell it for anything over £100 and make a profit.

---

[4] Do you get a sense that I have some mild PTSD (post-traumatic stress disorder) here? Or perhaps PHSD (post-handbag stress disorder)?

10 THINGS I ~~HATE~~ LOVE ABOUT MONEY

Imagine I have two consumers who want the bag. One is reckless, wants it straight away and is quite willing to pay £500 for it. The other one is thoughtful, not in a hurry and will only pay £200 for it.

Both customers are profitable, but the retailer would be foolish to price the bag at £200. Far better to price it at £500:

- Where people who are willing to pay £500 are going to shop.
- On release when reckless people will pay a premium to buy it because they want the new thing.

Then price it at £200:

- In the discount store or in a sale.[5]
- Later, when the product is no longer on the front cover of *Vogue*.

This means that the bag manufacturer gets an average price of £350 (and therefore a profit of £300 for two bags sold) rather than an average price of £200 (and therefore a profit of only £100).

This is true for goods and services right across the spectrum.

There is a (no doubt apocryphal) tale of a pizza joint (which will remain nameless) which gives out coupons left, right and centre with an expected average price of 60% of MSRP across all channels. One day someone came in and actually paid full price for a pizza and the manager fainted with shock.

The simple fact is, there are consumers who are very demanding and want the best deal. These people will negotiate, barter, and hunt around until they find the best price. They can be picky, but they also spend a lot of money, so shops still want to sell to them.

Have you seen how many discounts are actually available for major stores? It's amazing.[6] The stores aren't stupid, they are simply targeting different price points at different demographics.

---

[5] Bicester Village anyone?
[6] See HyperJar if you don't believe me.

Retail Inefficient Market Hypothesis #2: Retailers expect different people to pay different prices, it's built into their business models and they expect it. Be part of the group who pays less.

Why Shops Sometimes Operate at a Loss

There are many times when businesses sell products at a loss. They do this for several potential reasons:

1. A product isn't selling well, and they want to get rid of it. Better to make some money from it rather than to simply chuck it in the bin.
2. A new version of the product is being released soon, and they want to clear old inventory in a specified time. You'll see this often when some electronics, like wireless headphones, go on sale at the same time at every retailer. A new model is likely coming soon.[7]
3. They included selling a percentage of a product at a loss as part of their calculation of average price above. Better to overstock and be more profitable with the occasional bargain, than undersupply, sell nothing at a loss but make less money.
4. To grow market share, a business may sell a product at a loss to win new customers before eventually increasing prices. This is a common strategy used by startup businesses.[8] It is entirely logical but presents incredible opportunities for consumers because goods and services are essentially being subsidised by venture capital investors.
5. Loss leaders. These are products that businesses intentionally sell at a loss either in the hope of securing your future business, or hoping you buy other more profitable products alongside them. You will see this every week when you shop at Tesco or Asda or Sainsbury's

---
[7] Here it is helpful to be on top of market gossip and chatter. I'll show you how to do this, I love it.
[8] Think Uber and Starbucks.

(but not Lidl or Aldi). The end of the aisle, or more prominent price tags. Brands such as Nestlé will offer products at a massive promotion in return for prime real estate. This can be done to grow sales or to try and introduce new customers to an item.
6. Financial trouble. A business that is struggling may need to offload most of its inventory so they will lower prices to move it. To carry inventory is expensive because it requires capital to do so. Imagine a shop has 1,000 MacBooks and each one cost them £1,000. That's £1,000,000 of inventory. Expensive.
7. Quarterly and annual earnings targets and other stupid financial metrics. Many companies are judged, at least in the short to medium term, on numbers which in the long term make no sense, like sales growth, or annual recurring revenues (rather than actually making profits). If a business needs to sell more TV sets in a given year to meet some revenue target, they may offer major discounts.

Retail Inefficient Market Hypothesis #3: There are plenty of reasons why a retailer may offer you a genuine bargain. You have no idea why. But take it.

The Mystery of Teaser Rates and Signing on Bonuses

For lots of services which require either subscriptions or repeated payments, merchants, utilities, and credit providers will offer 'teaser rates' or 'signing on bonuses'. Examples:

- Subscribe and get the first three months free.
- Zero interest on credit card transfers for 12 months.
- Lower mortgage rates for the first few years.
- Higher bank interest rates or cashback for a period of time.

What on earth is going on? Well, they have done the maths. Gaining a long-term customer has a value of £X. Paying a teaser rate has a value of £Y. The number of people who will take the teaser rate or signing on bonus then switch again is Z%. The merchant or utility has simply worked out that Z is sufficiently low (since they lose money on people who switch repeatedly) and that X > Y when adjusted for Z. What does this mean?

- Switching (being 'part of the Z') has real value.
- People who don't switch moan about new customers getting a better rate.
- Martin Lewis and Money Savings Expert have lots of great advice about what to do.

Having worked in the mortgage industry I have to confess to having some sympathy with companies who provide teaser rates. What exactly is the alternative? If you don't you won't get any new customers and lots of your customers will switch. It's damned if you do, damned if you don't, but the fact remains:

Retail Inefficient Market Hypothesis #4: You can get better deals because your fellow customers fail to do so.

So let's summarise these four facts about the inefficiency of the retail market:

- Most retailers don't expect everyone to pay full price.
- There are reductions to be had almost everywhere.
- If you don't take them, you are subsidising others who do.

So What Kind of Shopper Are You?

Let's think how a hypothetical retailer might now group its customers.

We have the **Bargain Hunters**. They don't miss any discount. They can be annoying, but they can also be relied upon for some revenue if the retailer needs it. They will spend hours researching prices, they know every loyalty scheme, they never let a coupon expire and they use cashback like it's toothpaste.[9]

Next, we have the **Switched-on Shoppers (SOS)**. SOS like a deal similar to bargain hunters, but it's not their everything. They will do a bit more research for expensive purchases but can't be bothered with swiping their loyalty card every time they shop at Snow and Rock or Pret. They will sometimes, though. They're just busy and distracted with life. Nothing wrong with that.

We have the **Clueless**.[10] These are the people who don't really care about what they pay for things. There can be many reasons: ignorance; being busy; or being sufficiently well off it doesn't matter. Either way, retailers love them the most because they can squeeze out the maximum margin.

Lastly, we have the **Casuals**. They sit between the Clueless and SOS. They don't really use loyalty programmes unless it's Tesco Clubcard (and that's because it's almost forced upon you – I know people who refuse to get a Clubcard because they are stubborn). They care about getting a good deal but are entirely passive about it. If you tell them about a deal, they will take it but they won't seek it out. They are on the cusp of saving lots of money but won't get there without some intervention.

To recap, from most active to least active spenders we have:

1. Bargain Hunters
2. Switched-on Shoppers (SOS)
3. Casuals
4. Clueless

Which type are you? It matters less where you lie within this spectrum, but you should know what kind of spender you are.

---

[9] I'm a big believer in dental hygiene here so I assume you are all brushing your teeth at least twice per day. Can you tell my children to do it more regularly please?

[10] Please don't be offended if this is you. It was me. It is a great deal of us.

Hopefully now that you understand how stores price their goods and know that they are motivated to offer deals, you can feel more comfortable about picking up what is on offer, and as we have discussed earlier in the book, it's amazing how stuff adds up.

This is the situation in a nutshell. Retailers use discounts to try and change behaviour. Because people are how they are, they can distribute offers quite broadly and not worry about everyone taking them up. If everyone took up their offers, they'd lose money. It's the law of averages working to our advantage. MSRP gives retailers flexibility to play with promotions and discounts to influence behaviour.

At HyperJar we estimate that there are easy annual savings from smart spending of over £2,646 for the average household. As you can see by plugging this into the tables in Chapter 2, this could add up to over a million pounds, if it was invested over a lifetime. If you are wealthy enough to afford this then that is fine, but do go into it with your eyes wide open.

WHERE THE DISCOUNTS ARE (AND HOW TO FIND THEM)

We know why retailers provide discounts, now let's start looking at specifics.

The most important point to remember is that retailers offer discounts in order to encourage you to spend. You always have to balance:

- Taking a discount on something you plan to buy anyway.
- Buying something you were not going to buy because there is a discount.

Let's focus on the former rather than the latter.

Broad-Based Discounting

Broad-based discounting (BBD) schemes provide discounts across many businesses and have specific reasons for existing.

BBD are useful when we look at stacking. Stacking is the art of using multiple discounts in one transaction. Retailers hate stacking for obvious reasons, but if it's allowed, we're going to take advantage of it.

Here are the most common forms of BBD:

- Cashback.
- Gift vouchers.
- Universal card point schemes.

There's usually little downside to exploring these types of offers and making them a part of your regular routine.

Cashback

Cashback is an interesting one. There are sites and services that will let you get cashback just by buying an item through a link. It's almost always internet based although recently there have been some card-linked cashback offers. Card-linked means you spend with your card, and if it has been registered with the cashback site, it will automatically recognise the retailer and the card and give you your cashback (eventually, you hope). Cashback gives you a percentage of your purchase back when you shop. Let's look at a real example. Topcashback is the biggest cashback site in the United Kingdom. In October 2024, Boots said that I could get 6% cashback on my purchases. So, if I spent £100, I would get back £6. Cashback can take a long time to appear in your account, sometimes up to six months. The delay is to ensure you haven't returned any of the items. You can imagine what would happen if businesses paid out cashback immediately, even if you returned all the items. It would be a clever way to earn some free money.[11]

To earn the cashback, you have to have cookies turned on with your browser and you need to navigate to the retailer website directly from the cashback site. This way it is all linked to your account.

Cashback amounts will vary but commodity services such as fuel and grocery will pay far less (or not at all) compared to products like clothing or roadside assistance. For example, AA breakdown service will offer as much as £150 cashback for people who sign up to a new annual policy.

There are multiple services that provide cashback. The market is led by Topcashback, Quidco and Rakuten, followed by numerous smaller services including HyperJar. There are also browser plug-in tools that will provide cashback, and one of the biggest is Honey, now owned by PayPal.

If you use cashback well, you can easily earn £100+ a year on shopping you already do.

Gift Cards or Gift Vouchers

Everyone knows what a gift card is and how it works. There are a few multi-retailer gift cards, but let's stick to the single shop example first. Almost every major brand has a gift card division, and their job is to try and sell gift cards. They sometimes sell directly via their website and in stores, but they also sell through third parties. You can buy gift cards for Amazon at Tesco. Digital gift cards are sold to third parties at a significant discount. In the old days, the third party would buy their aggregate £1,000,000 worth of gift cards for £900,000 and then sell them to consumers for the face value, earning a £100,000 profit in this example. But what has happened more

---

[11] And make a shop go bankrupt. There are some great examples of promotions which have gone wrong in the past. Look up the Hoover free flights promotion if you want some amusement.

recently is third parties will sell these gift cards and give some or all of this discount back to the consumer. It's these opportunities we want to take advantage of because the savings can be enormous.

Gift cards have a few key differences compared to cash back.

- Gift cards typically offer a larger discount, especially with supermarkets.
- Gift cards offer the discount immediately, no cookie tracking or waiting period required.
- Gift cards can expire at which point they are worthless.
- Gift cards can be stacked with any other discount or reward. For cashback this isn't always the case.
- Gift cards, even digital ones, can be used for physical shops. I can buy Aldi gift cards, but I cannot do Aldi cashback.
- Gift cards carry risk because if the shop goes bankrupt before you spend it, you will likely lose your money.

If I were to buy a Nike gift card directly, I'm not going to get any discount. You need to buy it from a third-party provider that is choosing to give some of the discount back to you. There are now multiple businesses doing this.[12] You simply find the gift card page, buy the gift card and you will be given a bonus for doing so.

Retailers sell gift cards at a discount for two primary reasons:

- A belief they can capture new customers with gift cards so there's a potential long-term value.
- An ability to earn significant margin from a phenomenon known as breakage. Breakage is when a customer forgets or loses their gift card and thus doesn't redeem it. If you have a £100 gift card and it expires, even though the shop sold that gift card for £90, by you not

---

[12] Of course including HyperJar.

redeeming it they were able to earn £90 for free. It is similar to teaser rates, so make sure you spend your gift cards.
- They can raise significant cash if a third-party is willing to buy large amounts in bulk.

Universal Card Point Schemes

Universal Card Point Schemes (UCPS) are any programme where you earn points simply by swiping your payment card. This does not include specific loyalty programmes so only universal ones such as Amex cards or other points-based banking cards. Most major banks offer different points and rewards. I have an HSBC credit card, and I earn points each time I use it. It's something like 1 point for every £1 spent and 100 points gives you £1 to redeem (that is to say, about 1%). The reason why these exist is because they are often used as marketing tools to entice you to use a certain card. Not surprisingly banks make money from you. You might as well take advantage of their free offers.

Next, we'll look at more shop specific discounts and loyalty schemes. Whenever an offer can be stacked, I'll be sure to point this out.

Retailer Discounts

Let's look deeper into store-specific discounts. These are discounts and deals that are very specific to a particular business. Many shops, especially online, offer coupons for your shopping. Online shopping is an extremely competitive world, and without much searching you can normally find discount codes for most shops. This is where the Honey plug-in really helps. When you go to checkout, the plug-in will automatically check if there are any discount codes. This is great for smaller e-commerce websites, but it even works on sites like Amazon and John Lewis. Discounts are often part of loyalty schemes (discussed in depth below). This could be a

Pets At Home loyalty plan where you get £10 off a bag of dog food coupon sent to you. It can be annoying signing up to a hundred different loyalty schemes, but it's usually worth your time.

Loyalty Programmes

I suspect everyone reading this is familiar with loyalty programmes, especially Tesco Clubcard, Sainsbury's Nectar and Boots Advantage. Most supermarkets have one, so do many other retailers. If you are like me, you have a wallet full of plastic. They all work quite similarly with a few exceptions. Usually, it involves swiping a card that gives you points for every £1 you spend, you can then redeem those points for in-store credit. The big ones have now moved into differentiated pricing.[13] At the moment every few weeks of regular shopping will earn you a few pounds of straight discount.

Personally, I don't love these loyalty schemes because I think they artificially obscure grocery prices. At the discounters, Aldi and Lidl, the price on the shelf is the price you pay and frankly it's usually cheaper.

Many businesses offer very similar reward schemes where you earn a point for every £1 you spend. As a rule of thumb, think of loyalty schemes as a 0.5–1% discount on your shopping.

Buy Now Pay Later

Lastly, we have the loyalty purchased though offering you credit. A low/no interest rate loan is subsidised by the retailer in order to make you buy something. It's the same discount to MSRP just paid to you in a different way which encourages debt. Use it with your eyes open – I'm not a fan of it at all.

Let's now look at some of the stuff to look out for. What about prices changing when you aren't really aware of it.

---

[13] For all the reasons we have discussed. They are betting on customers behaving differently.

Contract Services

Most of you will have multiple contracts for services you rely on – streaming, breakdown services, utilities, insurance.

When contracts end, the price almost always goes up – we have discussed why – but be careful to watch out for when teaser rates finish, when letters come round discussing new terms, or when annual insurance rates are up for renewal.

When you sign up for many services there is often a default setting to auto-renew your contract. In one sense this is convenient because you don't want your service to expire. However, more often than not, it is an opportunity for a provider to test if you are a Bargain Hunter, an SOS, a Casual or Clueless. The renewal price is rarely competitive compared to what you can find with a simple search on one of the main comparison sites.[14]

Something else to be mindful of are mid-contract price increases. This is becoming extremely common, and I find them very disappointing. Most broadband and mobile phone providers will write in annual contract rises of RPI or CPI + 3.8%.[15] And they all increase by approximately the same amount. The justification is to help cover the cost of their services and infrastructure. But in my opinion, that is what a business does. It charges a price in the market that will allow them to provide a service and return a profit. Some vendors advertise no mid-contract price increases; carefully check for this and incorporate that into the featured price to do a more accurate comparison. My hope is that if enough people do this the market will be forced to stop this annoying practice.

---

[14] I've had quotes for rollover insurance double what I could get doing a simple search. This simple exercise of checking prices saved me £500.

[15] The RPI (Retail Price Index) is an official measure of inflation that includes housing costs such as rent and mortgage payments. This is generally higher than the CPI (Consumer Price Index), which is a measure of inflation that excludes housing costs (along with some other differences including how it's precisely calculated). Historically, RPI is about 1% higher than CPI.

WHEN LOYALTY COUNTS: BULK BUYING; MERCHANT LOYALTY SCHEMES

Discounts and loyalty can give you value. The key is they are additive. You can get the points and free shipping and lower priced goods if you use them, so you should. But you must be disciplined. You must not change your intended behaviour.

Some of the trickiest situations are the ones that encourage you to buy multiple items for a reduced price. For simple items like food this is less of a concern because you can adjust your shop and meal planning and it's relatively short term.

Where you need to be very thoughtful is when it's for bigger items like clothing, hardware or sporting equipment. Do you actually need a second football? Or eight new plugs. Go back to your Cost Per Use calculation – second items have a very high CPU if they are not used.

With that said, buying in bulk can be advantageous if you plan ahead. This is especially true for consumable products. There is a real art to bulk buying.

I'm going to lay out some bulk-buying rules:

- Don't bulk buy perishable items unless you're absolutely certain you will consume them before they expire.[16]
- A bulk purchase must never put you into deficit. That is to say, never borrow money to bulk purchase.
- Do quick maths to determine if a bulk purchase makes sense. The price per unit needs to be lower, and you need to have confidence you'll use the entire stock of items and not change your usage. You'll

---

[16] And not because you plan to force feed yourself an ungodly amount of biscuits.

also need to spend that much less on your next shops to embed those savings.
- Do you actually have space for it?

Bulk buying can be great. If so, take advantage of it when you can. Places like Costco can have fabulous savings, as can websites like Amazon. But way too many people think bulk buying saves them more money than it actually does, it takes up space, and it is not the solution for forward planning that many people think it is.

If you want to hoard something, hoard your money. It's easier to store, and more useful than 50l of ketchup.

THE ART OF THE DELAY

You would be amazed how much money you can save from just spending money a little less often. This is especially true of technology where consumption is largely driven by upgrading devices to newer versions. The manufacturers know this, and most do everything in their power to make you throw away the old version and buy the shiny new one.

What Can We Not Delay?

Let's first think about spend that we cannot delay. We can't delay buying food. We need to eat and drink every day. We can't delay taking a fitness class (if we want to stay in shape). You have to pay for transport since you need to get to work or school and you need to pay your bills.

In general, we can't delay paying for necessities. Basically, the spend we deduct from our income in order to calculate our DON. But what about spend from your DON? It's this spending that has the potential to be delayed. A great deal of it can be delayed. We have discussed why extending

Phase 2 is a great idea from a habit-forming point of view but it can also save you real money.

What Can We Delay?

We can delay buying lots of things, and having this understanding can become a superpower. Our modern economy is predicated on encouraging people to buy stuff, and then more stuff, and then if you already have all the stuff, to upgrade to the latest stuff. We're going to look at when and how we can delay and the positive impact this will bring to your mind and money.

What are some examples of purchases we can delay?

- Consumer technology including smartphones, televisions and tablets.
- Home appliances including vacuums, toasters and food processors.
- Vehicles.
- Shoes and clothing.
- Hobby items such as crafts, games, sports kit.
- Entertainment including concert tickets, shows, club memberships.

So why should we try and delay purchases:

- For all the reasons previously discussed – it's good for teaching spending zen.
- Because prices of many goods simply go down over time.
- To lower our replacement frequency. It's amazing how much you can save by changing your kit less frequently.

Many fashionable items are sold with a very high MSRP compared to their actual cost of manufacture. This is for many reasons:

- Some (reckless) people want stuff as soon as it becomes available – welcome to Instagram.
- Some people are totally price insensitive.

- High (initial) prices imply quality and exclusivity. For luxury goods more expensive items restrict who can buy it or assume relative price equals relative quality.[17]
- Because high initial prices allow you to offer seemingly bigger discounts at a later point in time.[18]

Prices for lots of goods simply go down for all the reasons discussed. So, if you can wait, you can save a huge amount of money. Wait for clothes to show up on discount sites and wait until the next technology release is due, it doesn't take long.

Many items have an implied redundancy, or replacement, cycle which simply isn't reflected in the reality of their actual useful life. This discussion can't go any further without discussing the iPhone.

Apple has done a brilliant job of turning their smartphones into high-end fashion items with an implied annual renewal cycle, even if the phones are broadly all the same. Oh look, the perfect screen is even more perfect, the battery life is longer than the battery life I had absolutely no problem with, it is now even more capable of beating a grandmaster at chess when all I use it for is Candy Crush. The majority of changes are internal so it is not even like most people can tell you have a new phone. There are some clues between models, like three camera lenses on the back instead of two (indicating if you have a pro version or a regular version of the phone) but it's almost impossible to tell.

As of this writing, Apple has just released their latest iPhone 16. A new iPhone 16 Pro Max with 1 TB costs £1,599.00.[19] Apple will still sell brand new versions of older phones down to iPhone 14. But they don't sell older

---

[17] Hands up who sorts by price on Amazon and ignores all the cheap stuff.
[18] In many countries it is illegal to make up discounts. Items have to be offered at full price for a while (even if almost no-one buys them).
[19] Why £1,599 and not simply £1,600? Another classic marketing wheeze which seems to have persisted. It was normally in lower priced items where a £3.99 might feel more like £3 instead of £4 at first glance. But everyone seems to do it all price levels. Cars seems to be a prominent exception. I'm curious what would happen to Apple sales if they did charge £1,600 instead of £1,599. I can't imagine anyone changing their purchase decision because of that £1 and perceived price. Maybe one day a company will do a real-time experiment on high-end items and see what happens?

versions of their flagship Pro model as they want to keep that exclusive. Because of that we can see how Apple depreciates their handsets. Let's look at the Apple website as of October 2024 and compare the price of models they currently have on sale:

- iPhone 16 128GB – £799
- iPhone 15 128GB – £699
- iPhone 14 128GB – £599

This indicates a steady £100 decline on previous year handsets. But this doesn't tell the full story. A better indication of the actual market value of brand-new Apple phones is by looking at resellers of new handsets on eBay. Let's check the prices at the same time as the listed Apple prices but sold on eBay. These are all brand new with a manufacturer warranty.

- iPhone 16 128GB – £699
- iPhone 15 128GB – £599
- iPhone 14 128GB – £499

A couple of interesting observations here. First, you can get a new iPhone for £100 cheaper on eBay compared to Apple direct. This is brand new, sealed with a full Apple manufacturer warranty from a reputable seller. Then when you look at the older models, they are also £100 cheaper than buying direct from Apple's website. So, if we compare a brand-new iPhone 14 128GB on eBay with a buying a brand-new iPhone 16 128GB from Apple, there is a significant £300 savings. This gives a sense of how much one can save by delaying the upgrade cycle.

I read some recent research on Apple and artificial intelligence (AI).[20] AI, as we know, is a white-hot trendy subject, but what really stood out to

---

[20] Mike Wuerthele (2025) 'After Strong Earnings, Morgan Stanley Inches Up AAPL Target to $275', *AppleInsider*, 31 January, https://appleinsider.com/articles/25/01/31/after-strong-earnings-morgan-stanley-inches-up-aapl-target-to-275#:~:text=As%20part%20of%20Morgan%20Stanley's,enough%20to%20satisfy%20the%20analysts.

me was their analysis on upgrade cycles of phones – how dull is that? But it turns out that the impact of everyone upgrading their phone just a month or two earlier means billions on the bottom line for Apple. At the moment, the iPhone replacement cycle is 4.8 years. The research suggested that this will shorten to 4.7 years in 2025 and then to 4.4 years in 2026 because more people will want AI features rather than sticking with their 'old' phones.

What this number means is an average person will wait a few months less before they buy a new iPhone. This might not seem to be a lot, but for Apple, across hundreds of millions of customers, it adds up to incredible amounts of money. It's in Apple's interest to get you to upgrade sooner, even one month will make a huge impact to their bottom line.

My job is to make sure you're not the one contributing to the decreased replacement cycle and instead putting on pressure to increase the replacement cycle. Every month and year you can wait provides significant savings. More importantly, the longer you wait, the more cash you have to invest for the future and other fun things you can buy. If you repeat this pattern over a lifetime, it will equate to many thousands of pounds. Let's take an example of someone who buys a new iPhone every year from age 20 to 60, versus someone who is just below the average cycle and buys a new iPhone every five years. Let's assume they can sell their used £800 iPhone for £400 a year later. Let's assume the slow upgrader can sell their five-year-old iPhone for £100.

Super-upgrader spend: £800 × 40 − (£400 × 40) = £16,000
Slow-upgrader spend: £800 × 8 − (£100 × 8) = £5,600

Therefore, the slow upgrader saves almost £10,400 in this simple example which could be invested and easily doubled over that timeframe. Now what if that delayer also bought a two-year-old new iPhone instead of the latest model and did that every five years?

Slow-upgrader older device spend: £500 × 8 − (£100 × 8) = £3,200
This now increases the savings from £10,400 to £12,800.

10 THINGS I ~~HATE~~ LOVE ABOUT MONEY

So delaying iPhones can lead to serious savings without decreasing your quality of life.

FINDING THE CHEAPEST PRODUCTS AND SERVICES

OK, you aren't going to delay, you are going to buy something so how do you get the best price? This will vary by sector, so we'll take a look at each.

Supermarkets

It is very simple. I want to spend the least amount of money as possible to get what I want. If that is shopping at Tesco and using the Clubcard to get my discounts – great. But if I can shop at Aldi[21] and spend less money overall, that's what I should do.

Just look at points schemes as small discounts on your spend (as discussed, 0.5–1% is a good rule of thumb). Then compare prices. It is that simple.

The points shouldn't be viewed as anything separate. It's easy to get caught in a trap of chasing points. Some people, especially frequent flyers, chase points with an obsession that becomes entirely irrational.[22] There are certain benefits like status and perks, but rarely do they amount to enough to offset typical price comparison shopping. Your job at the end of the day is to just pay the lowest price possible.

---

[21] Disclaimer. I love Aldi. I love the store, I love the employees, I love the business. I love it more than Lidl who I don't love very much.

[22] I recently read an article in the *Wall Street Journal* about how the WNBA (a women's professional basketball league in the USA) has become so successful that players are now able to fly private charter jets instead of commercial. Many players are now upset about losing their airline points and loyalty (rather than about the climate issues, but let's not go there). Talk about misguided priorities. (Source: R. Backman [2024] 'These Athletes Now Fly Private. In One Way, That's a Downgrade', *Wall Street Journal*, 11 October, https://www.wsj.com/sports/basketball/wnba-finals-liberty-lynx-charter-travel-basketball-f9222dd3.)

Now let's talk about own label products, it is similar to money off vouchers. They are typically just selling the same stuff at a lower price based on demographic profiling. Products are often manufactured in the same factories as big brands. This will vary but the point is, don't think of store brand products as being necessarily inferior. It's worth taking time to taste test and compare. If you're able to make a switch from big brand to own label, you could easily save £50 in a single weekly shop – this is a huge amount over a year. My family loves ketchup. My daughter practically lives on it. Like most people we like Heinz. One shop, I decided to buy four different brands of ketchup to compare. What happened surprised me. One wasn't good, but the other three were all quite tasty and I could barely tell the difference. The best part? It was half price![23] Start making a concerted effort to replace big brand with own label and you can save thousands of pounds per year.

Shopping Around

You can go deep, but using the 80/20 rule, for non-related items which you can buy online, look to the holy trinity: Google, Amazon and eBay. I always do the following four steps (Figure 8.1) – it now comes as naturally to me as blinking.

Personally, I find, 9 times out of 10 you'll find your best price on eBay.[24] Sometimes Amazon will have the lowest price but usually only if there's a promotion. Many people get caught in the Amazon convenience trap. They have your details; you can buy almost anything, and Amazon's customer service is fabulous and convenient when things go wrong. The delivery speed is incredible. This convenience is worth something, but be aware of what it costs, especially for larger items.

---

[23] I'm planning to conduct objective tests of own label products myself to give people a sense of how an own label compares to a name brand label. This will come on my website so stay tuned! This would then serve as a handy reference to let people swap out items without worrying about something either tasting awful or underperforming.

[24] This was even more profound before Brexit when resellers in Europe could sell items for much cheaper.

Figure 8.1   It Really Is This Simple

A bit like spending, the obsession with getting stuff right now is getting to be a bit absurd. Can't you wait two or three days? Even if you are ordering on Amazon, it's probably better for you, and certainly better for the environment, to cluster your deliveries once a week (or less – yes, you can do this). Do you really need everything tomorrow?[25]

---

[25] Or indeed the same day. This still freaks me out – how is it even possible?

By the way, there is an art to buying on eBay. Rely on seller ratings. These are simple ratings where real customers can give feedback on their purchase experience with that seller. If a seller has no ratings, be careful. If they have thousands of positive ratings, you're going to be just fine.

Beware of Fraud

We have discussed why you shouldn't buy stuff the first time you see it advertised for a whole host of reasons but let's add another one. Fraud.

If you use Facebook or other social media tools, there are many fraudulent sellers and ads. Essentially if the price seems too good to be true it likely is. Lloyds Bank conducted research in 2023 which showed that two-thirds of all online shopping scams start on Facebook and Instagram – that's a scam once every seven minutes.

- If there aren't any independent reviews of a business stay away.
- Don't just follow links without thinking. It's often worth taking a break, then looking up the vendor yourself from a fresh browser.

Sales

Another strategy is delaying purchases until big sale events (like the January sales or more recently Black Friday). I'm not a strong proponent of this, because you're not guaranteed to see what you want on sale, and half of the purpose of these sales is to tempt you to waste your money on stuff you don't really need. But if you aren't in a rush, why not wait?

HONEY BROWSER PLUG-IN

For all your online shopping, in addition to the above tips, use a Honey plug in and it will automatically find the latest coupon code and discounts.

This obviously won't work for your instore grocery purchase, but for anything online it's quite good. It costs nothing and operates automatically so there is little downside.

Be aware that there is some controversy with the Honey plug-in, that it doesn't always offer you the best available discount due to potential conflicts of interest with paid partners. As always be vigilant!

RULE 8 WRAP-UP

This rule was all about what we need to do save the most money whilst doing our shopping.

There are a few key takeaways:

- A great deal of what you want to buy can be got at a lower price if you make a bit of an effort to find out how.
- This is actually part of the core business model of most retailers so don't be shy in looking for discounts and taking them.
- An average family can probably save thousands of pounds a year by focusing on buying goods and services cheaply. This is very material for most people, especially over many years.
- Delaying purchases, especially for technology or fashion, can save you thousands of pounds over your lifetime. This is because you will both buy less and be able to buy things for a better price. Try to incorporate this philosophy into as many purchase decisions as you can.

CHAPTER NINE

RULE 9: ENJOY THE JOURNEY (AND BUILD A SUNNY-DAY FUND)

Sorting your spending is fun on so many levels – for you and for those around you.

'It is not the man who has too little, but the man who craves more, that is poor.'

—*Seneca*

'If you work for a living, why do you kill yourself working?'
—*Tuco,* The Good, the Bad and the Ugly

What I hate – How not spending so much, is somehow seen as miserly, or wearing a hair shirt, as if you are denying yourself something.

What I love – How good it feels when you start getting in control of your spending and start to save. It actually feels good and when things feel good, they become infectious. Not spending money isn't a sacrifice, you get to spend it later – and wasting money is just stupid.

The thought of going for a run bores a lot of people. Going to the gym and lifting until your muscles hurt sounds painful. Why do people choose to do it? People do it because they know it's good for them, but also (and you may find this hard to believe) lots of people really enjoy it. I know. Now learning to love exercise doesn't usually happen overnight, but most people who get into a regular habit of physical fitness learn to love it.

The good news is the same is absolutely true with financial fitness. In fact, I reckon it is much easier to love, and faster to see results, than going to the gym.[1]

Financial fitness isn't about being a miser and taking the fun out of life. Quite the reverse:

- Every pound you don't waste you get to spend.
- Every pound you save grows in value and then you get to spend it later.
- Every pound you don't spend on something you don't really need you get to spend on something you will love.

So over time, it's all about spending more, on better and more important things.

This rule is about reinforcing why spending well is great. How it makes you feel, why delaying spending is exciting, and how it can change your interactions with others.

---

[1] But please do both. You knew I was going to say that didn't you?

Rule 9: Enjoy the Journey (and Build a Sunny-Day Fund)

First, let's talk about how mastering your spending can make you feel:

- You will feel more in control overall.
- You will enjoy every day more because you will lower near-term uncertainties.
- You will feel more optimistic about the future.
- You will experience 'double dopamine'.
- You get to be smug, when you see people who are financially unfit.[2]

BEING IN CONTROL IS COOL

Think about how you feel when you have a tidy house, when your holiday is all planned and everything is booked, or when all your homework is done.[3] Being on top of stuff just feels great. If you make a list of stuff that you need to do, you will probably be surprised how many of your to-do's are actually to do with money. Getting on top of your spending has a fantastic pay-out ratio when it comes to feeling in control. It's not too hard to do – once you have got into a reasonable equilibrium state it is even easier to stay there and takes very little time to do.

Being in control of how well organised your sock draw is feels good but is hardly existential. Being in control of your money is like being in control of your health – it is profoundly important and getting it right can make you feel like you have really got your shit together. It's fantastic.

---

[2] Yeah, maybe it's not an attractive trait, but it's the truth. It is enjoyable being better at something than most other people – and the vast majority of people have not got their financial house in order.
[3] I have obviously given this speech to my children. Let's see if I can do a better job with you.

ENJOY EVERY DAY MORE: MAKE EVERY DAY A SATURDAY

For many people there is a sense of excitement and optimism on a Friday which is in stark contrast to a nagging bit of dread on a Sunday afternoon and evening.[4] Why does this happen? It's because humans are always thinking about the future, even subconsciously.

This is the root of a huge amount of anxiety for many people, a level of uncertainty, even if it isn't true – let's face it, Sunday should be way better than Friday. Sunday is totally free; you can do what you want. Friday you're working.[5] If you aren't worried or thinking about the future at all, then Sunday is the same as Saturday (obviously the best day), and Friday is no different than Tuesday (obviously the worst day[6]).

The Sunday Scaries also happen with money. Most people have a constant nagging low-level subconscious process of worry about their current situation, exactly how much they have to get through the month, what can and cannot be afforded, something they are owed, a bill they know they need to sort out. It's messy stuff. There is nothing inherently wrong with these mental processes – it is part of the general survival instinct. That said, it's very easy to obsess a little too much, or worry a little too much about stuff which you aren't actually doing anything about. It's not good for us.

Getting on top of your money, having clear sight of the next month or two, knowing that you have enough – these are all great ways to remove lots of nagging worries and make every day feel like a financial Friday.

---

[4] This phenomenon is so common that it has its own name, the Sunday Scaries.
[5] I'm generalising about a typical office job worker or student. Apologies to retail, health and service workers and the many people who work on Sundays. I hope you can also relate to the sentiment I'm describing.
[6] Not just in my opinion, I took a show of hands around the office.

Rule 9: Enjoy the Journey (and Build a Sunny-Day Fund)

THE FUTURE

Enough about the weekend, let's talk about next year, or 10 years from now, or when you retire. Nothing feels worse than concerns about not having enough, either for day-to-day living or for having enough resilience to cope with a rainy day. Understanding and managing your money better has two major impacts on the future:

- Regardless of how much you save or invest, understanding how much you need for your day-to-day living costs and other expenses can give you a great deal more information about the future, and comfort that you will be able to get by – most people need less than they think.
- By saving small amounts you can build up funds for rainy and sunny days (see below).
- By investing small amounts over many years you can start to build a picture of what kind of retirement you are going to have. There is no point burying your head in the sand, unless you are fortunate enough to have a great defined benefit pension, most of us need to save a considerable amount of money if we want to have a very comfortable retirement. Once you can see even the pathway to a goal of saving a reasonable amount for retirement it can reduce long-term worries about the future substantially. We will talk more about investing, and how simple and enjoyable it can be in the next chapter.
- If you have a house, paying off your mortgage faster is one of the most satisfying things in the world. Having a mortgage-free house just feels great.[7]

---

[7] Ask a third of homeowners. That's roughly the percentage who own their houses outright without any mortgage. Staggering isn't it? I bet you would never have guessed that.

As we have shown, small amounts of regular savings can add up to big amounts of money in the future. Understanding how much you will need, how much you may need, and having an idea of how you are going to get to long-term financial goals is one of the most fulfilling, worry reducing and fabulous feelings you can have.

DOUBLE DOPAMINE: TWO FOR ONE

Dopamine is a hormone known as the 'feel-good' hormone because it gives people pleasurable sensations. Often when people spend money (especially when it's fun shopping), it is akin to a dopamine release. There is no point denying that shopping can be fun, The expression 'retail therapy' didn't come from nowhere. Now many of the bad habits we're trying to combat are due to this dopamine effect, but it doesn't mean that you can't get a similar, or better kick when you are spending well.

So let's embrace the dopamine hit, but in a more balanced and sustainable way. In fact, let's go all in and aim for what I call a double dopamine shopping hit.

We do this by adhering to the following simple two-step process:

- Save up for something.
- Buy the item later from the aforementioned savings.

That's right, it's honestly as simple as that. If you haven't done this before, let me explain what's happening.

Firstly, when you begin to save deliberately for a goal, that process becomes rewarding. Seeing a balance get larger, while anticipating the end result, is exciting – it almost feels like you are buying a little piece of the

Rule 9: Enjoy the Journey (and Build a Sunny-Day Fund)

item every time you put some money aside. It is like multiple small releases of dopamine.[8]

Secondly, when you do reach your goal and buy your item you get exactly the same dopamine hit you always get from shopping. But you know what, it's even better because it will almost feel like it was for free.[9]

There is a funny phenomenon that seems to happen when you set money aside from your regular spending channel for a future purchase. You kind of forget about it – you consider it spent. The more you automate your savings the more powerful this effect will be.

I'd also note that stuff you save up for is often fun (or very important), which makes the hit even bigger. It's similar to when you spend an Amazon gift card versus your money. Do you spend an Amazon gift card on some cleaning products that you need? I doubt it, you probably buy something a bit more fun.

Planning and saving for fun stuff lowers levels of guilt for being frivolous. Planning and saving can release much more shopping dopamine than a single reckless purchase. Even just delaying spend you know you are going to make with money you already have can have this effect. This feeling is good, we can all get used to it (and we're all going to because we're going to stick to these rules right?).

---

[8] The key to doing this well is having funds specifically segregated to your goal. I would recommend setting up a specific jar in HyperJar, but any modern banking app with separated containers will do the trick (albeit with less sophisticated functionality, but hey, not everyone can be HyperJar). I feel like a drug pusher.

[9] That is, if you even decide you still want to buy the item in question. This is the other advantage of setting up saving goals and working towards them. You often change your mind. Then you have money and no regret purchase, win-win.

BE SMUG

I don't really drink. In the past, my friends would try and get me to drink more than the occasional glass, and when I turned them down they would accuse me of 'not being fun'. Firstly, you can definitely have a lot of fun without a drink,[10] but secondly, as I watched my friends with their expanding waistlines, and listened to their moaning about hangovers and the cost of big nights out, it made me feel great (a nicer word than smug).

Money is the same; the vast majority of people have definitely not got their financial shit together. If you have, you are part of an exclusive club. Luxuriate in your membership. Cross the velvet rope and come inside. Think about all those poor unfortunates outside in the rain. And have a (non-alcoholic) drink with me. It will make you feel great. Slightly guilty, but great.

Now let's talk a bit about what you can do with any excess funds which can really make you feel wonderful (rather than just blowing them down at the pub).

A RAINY-DAY FUND

Unexpected stuff happens – a boiler blows up, you get ill, your friends and family need your help. Having some money set aside for rainy days feels great, even if you never use it.[11]

There is quite a lot of literature on rainy-day funds online – most of it suggests that you should have between three and six months of essential expenses locked away somewhere in a savings account.

---

[10] Thankfully a lot more people are realising this now than when I was growing up. God bless the younger generation.
[11] And let's hope you never have to. I'm always surprised when people say, spend all your money, you can't take it with you. Actually having money, with its theoretical potential to be used, for good times or bad times can be an entirely logical end in and of itself because of how it makes you feel.

Try and set up a rainy-day fund. It may be easy, or it may take a few years, it doesn't matter. The act of planning it will make you feel in control. When you have achieved it you will feel like a financial rock-star just knowing that it is there.

THE SUNNY-DAY FUND

Lots of people talk about rainy-day funds, why does no one talk about sunny-day funds?[12]

I mentioned sunny-day funds above (let's use SDF – you know I love my acronyms), but let's go into more detail. An SDF is money you've saved up and set aside with the express idea that it is there to do something fun. Have you always wanted to go to Tahiti for three months to drink cocktails, relax on the beach, eat delicious food and surf all day?[13] Have you always wanted a new Ducati Panigale V4S in classic red livery?[14] Maybe you want to finally go to Endo at the Rotunda and experience the best sushi of your life for a grand treat?[15] Perhaps you haven't worked it out yet, but there is no reason not to have an SDF for future use when the mood takes you.

So, the SDF is a tool you can use to achieve these goals – start saving money for fun, don't wait for the lottery win. The best thing about having an SDF is it's double dopamine again – the anticipation of using your SDF, for whatever purpose, is actually fun in and of itself. I've not had sushi at Endo (yet), but the thought of it is exciting and fun and I'm already looking forward to it, I have a plan. I can live with that. In fact, I could live the rest of my life never having sushi at Endo (sad) and still be a happy man. Anticipation is a powerful force. For most people, you have the advantage

---
[12] Finance does tend to lean towards miserable narratives. I guess fear sells financial products better?
[13] Okay maybe that's just me then. I'm going to do Tahiti and do it large one day.
[14] Okay maybe that's just me again?
[15] I hear it's the best sushi in London. I've promised myself a trip if this book actually sells. Me again.

10 THINGS I ~~HATE~~ LOVE ABOUT MONEY

of not owning a Ferrari, yet.[16] Many times, the journey can be more fun that the destination. There is an art to this. If something feels too far away, or almost impossible, it becomes less exciting. If you're young and single, would you be more excited about the thought of dating a pop star; or the person in your class that you've said hi to once who is really cute and charming, but you've been too nervous to speak to? Exactly, it's the one that's within reach.

You need to build an SDF that is ambitious yet within reach, and you need to constantly adjust this as you begin to achieve, and your dreams expand. This can happen at any age and at any level of wealth, it doesn't matter – goals are goals.

A bigger yacht, an education fund for grandchildren, a charitable endeavour. Anyone can eliminate waste, build new ambition and create an alternate future.

Let's break down the sunny-day fund goals and steps:

1. Make the changes in our lives feel fun and exciting, so we stick with them. An SDF is a great way to get a pay-out for all the lessons in this book, however small it is.
2. Make an SDF exciting, you need to believe you can achieve it.
3. Try and fund the SDF regularly, every time you fund it you will feel great.
4. Re-evaluate the objectives of your SDF regularly, or have open ended goals, the key point is to know that it is money you are setting aside for fun and fulfillment, not for buying toilet paper.
5. Talk about your SDF with your close friends and family. It will help you stick to it, and who knows, they might set one up too.

---

[16] Three things here. Firstly, I hope some of my readers do own a Ferrari already; secondly, I apologise for this very juvenile male list of objects, I do need to balance it out; and thirdly, have you ever considered just borrowing one and getting it out of your system? Any readers who do have a Ferrari, please get in touch.

Rule 9: Enjoy the Journey (and Build a Sunny-Day Fund)

6. Try to have both a sunny- and a rainy-day fund. Obviously if you absolutely need to use your SDF in an emergency, it is there. But too many people treat all savings as fungible, and spend their SDF so often, it might as well not be there.[17]

PLANNING FOR RETIREMENT

At some point you stop earning and you are only spending. Clearly, spending well becomes an even more important skill in this phase of your life. Saving up for retirement is great, but you would be surprised how much you actually need, and with how little savings most people manage.

Let's talk about how much you actually need. A *Which?* survey in 2023 found that a couple in retirement need about £19,000 per annum for essentials, £28,000 if they want to include some leisure spending, and £44,000 if they want to include luxuries such as extended long-haul holidays.

How much do you need to save up to earn an income of £44,000? Well there is a good rule of thumb that you can spend about 4% of your savings per year. This means that a couple needs to put away close to a million pounds in order to achieve this in retirement.

It seems impossible doesn't it? But as we have said before, even if you can't save such a huge amount, small regular savings and investments soon add up.

Have a plan for retirement, think about it now. Even if you can't save a million, every little helps, and being on top of it, rather than ignoring it or

---

[17] Have you seen the film *Up*? Where Carl and Ellie have an SDF for getting to Paradise Falls which they are constantly spending on other essential stuff, and they never get there before Ellie dies? Reader, I wept buckets. Don't be Ellie.

kicking the can down the road, makes a real difference, both in the future, and also to your current levels of worry and happiness. I talk more about investing money in the next chapter.

CHECK IN ON YOURSELF

How do we stick to the plan every day? How do we keep the motivation to keep doing these activities and making this journey enjoyable? How do we make a rainy Tuesday in the office feel like Saturday?

You have to check in on your progress and be proud of yourself, give yourself a pat on the back. Too often people work towards a goal and don't check in and give themselves any credit for what they have achieved.

You need to check in, and you need to celebrate tiny wins. It's one of the reasons why I recommend saving as often as possible. Do you know that most people who invest in ISAs only do it once a year around the start/end of the tax year? Where is the fun in that? Not only is it hard to plan, but you are also literally unnecessarily starving yourself of financial dopamine.

Once you have your system, try to check in on your savings weekly, it only takes a few seconds. I don't want you becoming obsessive, but watching numbers get bigger is very satisfying.[18] I'm jumping a bit ahead of myself – we haven't talked about how we put this excess to work exactly. That is the topic for Rule 10. But a sneak preview, make micro transfers to savings as often as possible. These micro transfers are getting us closer to our goals.

Check your habits; use time in Phase 1 spending to look at what you have done and when it works, feel good about it. Celebrate making fewer impulse purchases. Reward yourself by sticking the money in your SDF.

---

[18] It's like getting on the scales when you are shedding a little weight, but much easier not to backslide.

Feel good about saying no to something you didn't really want to attend anyway.

All these things that you weren't doing before, give yourself credit for them now.

IT ISN'T JUST REPETITION THAT MAKES THINGS STICK

Repetition makes things stick. Have I mentioned this before?

It's a proven formula and it also works with spending – it is one of the purposes of having an SDF (it is not just for the sushi) and it is why we are going to regularly check in on our progress.

But there is a really important third point, we're going to socialise what we're doing with our close friends and family.

People may earn salaries, deposit and borrow money individually[19] but most people spend together.[20] Seventy per cent of the population lives in households with more than one person – a partner, children, parents, flatmates, friends.

Given that you spend with your family and friends, and we have discussed at length the challenges surrounding this, it makes sense to try and get your nearest and dearest involved in building good habits – both to keep you on track, but also because it is important for them too.

One of the reasons why gyms are popular is that being around other people exercising is motivating. For most people, going for a walk or a bike ride is much more fun (and therefore much more likely) when there are other people to do it with.

---

[19] That is as far as the analysis of most banks go – which is why bank accounts are for individuals.
[20] Social spending is at the very heart of my app HyperJar.

Money is different, it's very personal and typically very private. People don't walk around talking about their financial situations.[21] So how do we socialise our journeys?

SOCIALISE YOUR NEW LIFESTYLE WITH YOUR SOCIAL CIRCLE

We need to look at what we are doing with our spending and somehow expand it into our social network. This may sound awkward, but there is a way to do this that won't be seen as obnoxious and will help you in your quest. I mentioned how the gym environment becomes motivating for exercise. Libraries are great places to study and read as they are quiet, and many other people are doing the same thing. Schools and universities are often just as much about being around many people learning the same thing as you, as they are about the actual teaching and tuition. There is no similar environment for your finances and spending. If you go into a bank, it's not a community. It's a place where you do your transactions, and you want privacy around your business.

We need to create an environment of your trusted friends and family. This becomes a community, a support group, a cheerleading section. If you can do this successfully, you massively increase your chances of success. If done well, you will also inspire and motivate other people to also become their best spending selves.

---

[21] Instagram bragging doesn't count. Wow, it's tedious, will there come a day when collectively the world gets bored of it?

Rule 9: Enjoy the Journey (and Build a Sunny-Day Fund)

Be confident in what you are doing, and don't be afraid to tell people. Back to the pub analogy again, it's so much easier when you say: 'No I'm not drinking, I have come off the sauce for a while because I need to get fit' – it actually feels great when you say it, when you own the narrative – all of a sudden it becomes a 'thing'. You are in control. Dry January anyone?[22] What are some equivalent statements that you might make about money:

- I'm not doing that since I'm trying to simplify my life.
- Look at my old iPhone, why did you get a new one?
- I've just done (insert great use of SDF here). It was great, I put money aside for it for the last six months.

You understand what you're doing and why you're doing it, so become a mini expert. Why not charm and delight your friends with some of the lessons from this book?[23] God knows enough people talk drivel about finance (and other stuff) so you will fit right in. The good news is that you will actually be talking sense.

Speak to your closest friends and family about your journey, the specifics, what your goals are. It is often much easier to get to your destination in any activity you choose to pursue with some encouragement. This also means that when you are doing something stupid, there is a good chance that they are going to tell you, and it will be easier for them to understand why you might be turning down that invite or being more organised about splitting bills. You will enjoy showing them that you can do this.

If you're a parent, this is a wonderful thing to discuss with your kids, it will also set them up for great habits when they get older (see Bonus Rule 11).

---
[22] I'm writing this paragraph on Christmas Eve. It can't come soon enough.
[23] Not too often. You don't want to be a bore. My excuse is that it is my job, so I get a free pass.

STOP THE TOXICS IN THEIR TRACKS

When you socialise what you're doing, some toxic people might view it as kryptonite.

People who tend to borrow money off you, look at you as a safety net or expect you to spend your money on them without concern for your finances[24] will start to think twice.

The best thing here, especially if you are Accepting or shy, is setting out what you are doing in advance completely takes the heat out of uncomfortable situations when they occur. If someone knows in advance of that expensive meal that you are serious about splitting the bill, it is far harder for someone to duck it when it actually happens.

Putting potentially toxic influences in their proper place feels great.

LET'S POPULARISE A WORD: THOIL

Thoil is a Yorkshire word which I only recently learned about as I researched this book. It means:

Someone being able to afford something, but not being able to justify the expense.

It's a wonderfully specific word, very subtle, and so very Yorkshire, and it's a wonderful philosophy that I wanted to include in this section on making things stick.[25]

---

[24] If my kids are reading this, I'm talking about you.
[25] My life will be complete if we can all make the word thoil a new 'thing'.

Rule 9: Enjoy the Journey (and Build a Sunny-Day Fund)

Have you ever looked at the (outrageous) price of something, and just felt that by buying it you would feel a bit ripped off? The £10 pint? The crazy expensive starter? The bonkers cost of parking near a beach?

It doesn't matter how much money you have (a millionaire can still be irritated by a £10 lager) at some point saying no, I can't thoil this, I'm not going to do it, can be an absolute pleasure. It's about being strong. It's about not letting the world take advantage of you. Who do they think they are, trying to pull the wool over your eyes, eh?

When you have a little money (and hopefully this book is going to help get you there) it's so easy to become more relaxed about money and therefore a little careless and profligate, but I'm telling you, overspending on stuff feels bad no matter what. Don't be a mug. If you can't thoil it don't do it.

Having a confidence that you can afford something and choose not to, without having to explain to people, is a superpower. Embrace it and use it; and use the word *thoil* with wild abandon.[26]

TRY AND BE HAPPY WITH WHAT YOU HAVE

One of the best things about getting older is that my ambitions are narrowing. I'm increasingly comfortable with what I have. My friends and family. Good food, nice walks, a fulfilling job – that is about it. When I was younger I wanted so much more.[27]

The sheer relief of not wanting an expensive lifestyle is one of the best things that can possibly happen to you. I look at all the yachts, supercars, and watches and it leaves me entirely cold.[28]

---

[26] People will look at you strangely and almost no-one will understand you. Yet.
[27] Cars and castles.
[28] Well actually it's another thing I feel pretty smug about.

Let's try a thought exercise: I call this thought exercise the £5 million conundrum. It's a very simple exercise, but it's much harder than you think.

Imagine tomorrow you woke up and all of a sudden £5 million appeared in your bank account. What would you do?

- Would you quit your job?
- Would you tell your friends?
- Would you move home?
- Would you start a business?
- Would you buy some things or travel?
- How would you spend and invest that money to make it last?

What are your actual long-term goals? You may find that the ones you really care about are a lot more achievable than you think. What are mine?

- Have a big rainy-day fund so I can make sure me and my family are as safe as possible from any nasty turns of events.
- Make sure I have enough to have a good retirement, especially if I get ill.
- Have a bigger house.
- As a bonus, maybe buy one incredible motorbike.

That's it. I'm simply not that ambitious. It's all achievable. I might be able to spend that £5 million somehow but it's actually pretty hard for me to work out how.

I have two friends, both very well off, both having had long 30-year careers in the city, both are married, both have lovely houses right in the middle of London. Their attitudes to life couldn't be more different:

- One is ridiculously happy about his financial situation, feels blessed at being in the 0.1%, drives a 20-year old Subaru[29] which he loves,

---

[29] Impreza WRX Turbo STI. What a car.

eats whatever he likes, goes on holiday to wherever he likes, cycles his bike, and plays video games. He is completely fulfilled. I'm sure he couldn't find a way to spend the £5 million if he tried – probably give most of it away.
- The other is always sad and depressed. He looks at others who have more than he does and feels that he is a failure. His Porsche 911 is five years old – he badly wants a new one. On holiday, if he isn't staying in a five-star hotel he feels terrible. When he visits friends' country houses who have even more money he is envious and depressed.[30]

They have the same amount but one is happy and one is sad. Think about what you would do with £5 million as an exercise in thinking about what is important to you.

EXPLORE YOUR MINDSET

So much of the journey is mostly a mindset. The £5 million conundrum exercise is an example of this. So much of how you perceive your spending journey will come down fundamentally to your identity and how you see yourself.

Look at the labels in Figure 9.1.

The odd thing about all of the labels, apart from the ones in the bottom right quadrant, is that while many of them are often the opposites of each other, they all seem to have a negative connotation, depending on who you're asking. You can't win – most words to describe people on the basis of their money are pejorative.

---

[30] Rather than thinking, hey, free accommodation, food and booze.

Figure 9.1   Financial Words Used to Describe People

In fact, when it comes to money, it becomes very difficult to think of a positive label except for one circumstance, the bottom right hand labels – when you're giving your money to someone else. All these words evoke immediate positive impressions. I find this interesting.

What seems to be missing are any labels for people who manage their money well. I'm sure there is some kind of deep meaning behind this, but I'll be damned if I know what it is.

There is nothing wrong with using money to live a better life, to enjoy your time on earth, to do as you please, to take care of your family, to work towards bigger goals.

What I do know is that as a society we have almost no positive personas that you can apply to someone who follows the lessons in this book. So let's make one up.

Think of yourself as a maestro. Become a **money maestro**.

Spending well, as we've learned is more art than science. Embrace this artistry. It is much more interesting than thinking about numbers and pounds and pence, and as we have seen, there is so much more to it than some kind of simple prescriptive method. Spending well is about understanding and numbers, but it is also about mindfulness, personality and happiness. There is an art to this, and to be a great artist requires thought and practice.

RULE 9 WRAP-UP

Spending well can be the source of a huge amount of happiness, and it can be great fun. Recognising this is an end in and of itself, but it will also make it far more likely you will stay the course until the habits become part of you.

The most important takeaways of Chapter 9 are:

- Make this process into an enjoyable lifelong journey. Start by building a sunny-day fund (SDF). An SDF is a fund that is in addition to a rainy-day fund, but instead of being for emergencies, it's for something you're excited about in the future, such as a vacation.
- Take advantage of double dopamine. This is the phenomenon of experiencing joy when you save and then again when you use those savings to buy something.
- Embrace your inner thoil. Take pride in being able to afford things but choosing not to because it's not the best thing for your situation.
- Think of yourself as a money maestro and avoid all the negative connotations associated with common money labels. This way you can feel empowered to make the decisions that work best for you and avoid society's labels.

CHAPTER TEN

RULE 10: BEGIN SAVING AND INVESTING DAILY

You're in the black, now let's put this to work.

'October. This is one of the particularly dangerous months to speculate in stocks. The others are July, January, September, April, November, May, March, June, December, August, and February.'

—*Mark Twain*

'Beware the investment activity that produces applause; the great moves are usually greeted by yawns.'

—*Warren Buffett*

What I hate – Investing is perceived as being something so complex that either you need to be wealthy before you can start, or you need to pay through the nose for expert help as it's too complex for the average person. None of this is remotely true.

What I love – You can start investing today with as little as £1. It's simple, it's really easy to do yourself, and it makes you feel fantastic and in control.

For every book I've read on fitness, I've probably read two on investing. Even if you ignore the pink newspaper which talks about nothing else very much, every regular paper usually has a section on personal finance. There are about 31,000 financial advisors in the UK, compared to 67,000 personal trainers.[1] Wow it must be complex (and boring). It's not, it's simple (and exciting).

For most people, investing is all about putting money away for the far distant future, for when you retire. This is basically true, but what is less talked about is that it makes you feel in control, and it makes you feel great right now, just like spending well.

For most people investing is a chore, something you do one day when you are a bit older, or something you do once a year because someone tells you to. It isn't, it's very easy – you have some money, make it grow faster whilst you are asleep. Doesn't that sound fun?

If you have created any sort of surplus, however small, put it to work so it keeps working while you are doing your 'thing'. As you know by now, I'm a big believer that getting going today, not tomorrow, is how we live our best lives.[2]

---

[1] Sources: A. Austin (2024) 'Worry for Profession as Young Adviser Numbers Plummet', *Financial Times Adviser*, 12 March, https://www.ftadviser.com/your-industry/2024/03/12/worry-for-profession-as-young-adviser-numbers-plummet/; D. Clark (2025) 'Estimated Number of Fitness and Wellness Instructors in the United Kingdom from 4th Quarter 2021 to 3rd Quarter 2024', *Statista*, 30 January, https://www.statista.com/statistics/319319/number-of-fitness-instructors-in-the-uk/.

[2] 'Just Do It' – Nike. A quote from earlier in the book. I wonder what would have happened if Scottish Widows had used that as a slogan rather than a lady in a black cape?

I'm not going to give you specific advice,[3] I'm going to talk about some general principles, it's what I do. I have come across many very wealthy people.[4] Apart from a few who make a sport of investing (and it doesn't always work), most of them do some variation on what is set out in this chapter with most of their money, despite what the media would have you think.

WHAT IS INVESTING ANYWAY?

If you don't need your money now, you might as well put it to work. If you stuff cash under your mattress for years, it will almost certainly be worth less when you take it out than when you stuffed it. Why? Inflation. £1 in 1924 would have the equivalent spending power as £78 would have today,[5] so that £1 you hid away would be worth basically 1p. Depressing.[6]

Now conversely, let's say you invested £1 in the US stock market in 1924 it would be worth approximately £14,000 today. So it comes down to this, would you rather have 1p or £14,000? Exactly.

Lots of people use the word investing in different ways, which is one of the reasons it all gets a bit confusing. For the purposes of Rule 10 I think of investing as:

- Putting your money to work for the long term.
- Having a sensible strategy where once you have invested your money you need to do very little ever again.

---

[3] It does depend on your circumstances, everyone has different requirements, just like spending. Also, I don't want to get locked up by the Financial Conduct Authority (the FCA).
[4] Some good some bad. But this is a book about money, so let's put that aside and see how they invest.
[5] I remember when a packet of Polos cost less than 5p. How old am I?
[6] Why don't I talk about the UK stock market? We will get to that, suffice to say, most of the really big companies in the world are in the US.

I say this to differentiate investing from trading and gambling.

- Trading is where you actively buy and sell investments such as shares in a relatively regular fashion to try and beat the market. Trading well involves a lot of expertise, research, work and not a small amount of luck.
- Gambling is where you go to the casino or the bookies and place a bet. You can do this with shares and investments as well – lots of people buy bitcoin for exactly this reason, a desire to get huge, short-term gains.

I don't recommend trading and gambling as the basis for any sort of long-term investing strategy. By all means trade, or gamble for fun with money you can afford to lose, but it's not a necessary part of any sensible strategy. We want to go with a plan which is nice and simple and will get us great returns over a nice long time frame.

So here are our first two principles:

- First, time (and compounding) is your friend. If you can, any gains you make on investments should be reinvested (easy if you have invested in a fund, they will do it for you) and over time this will have a major impact.
- Second, you don't need to think about having a complicated investment strategy. You don't need to keep switching around, this is trading (gambling) not investing.[7]

---

[7] Very few people can do this and win. I'm 50, I've met about three people. They may have just been very lucky, I'm not sure.

THREE TIME FRAMES

I like to think about three time frames:

- **Short**: Basically, your day-to-day spending money. Your salary or other money you have to cover off your normal expenses over the next month or two. Let's go for 1–5 months.
- **Medium**: Money you are setting aside for larger expenses, your rainy-day fund, your sunny-day fund(s), saving up for a deposit. Let's go for 1–5 years.
- **Long**: Money you are putting away for the long term, probably for retirement. Let's go for 5–50+ years.

I am going to propose a different investment strategy for each of the three time frames.

THREE INVESTMENTS

The noise surrounding possible investments is just spectacular. Everybody has some sort of scheme or idea that they will tell you is going to make you rich (for a nice big fee), or some sort of complex strategy that they will kindly manage for you (for a nice big fee). I personally focus on just three investments:

- **Cash**: Put money in a savings account with as high an interest rate as possible.
- **Houses**: Buy yourself a house. It's fun, you get to live in it and not pay tax on any gain.
- **Shares**: Buy shares in companies. For most people, you can do this through pension schemes or ISAs, which means you won't pay any tax on gains here either.

Most people understand cash and houses. Shares[8] are simply a 'share' in a company. An example:

- Marks & Spencer has 1,963,500,000 shares outstanding.
- So, if you own 1,000 M&S shares you own 0.000051% of the company.
- You are entitled to 0.000051% of the profits.[9]

People have opinions on how good companies are, and how much profit they are probably going to make. These opinions change all the time, so the value of any given share goes up and down accordingly.

But which shares to buy? Don't bother to try to work it out, that's trading, just buy a fund (or two):

- A fund is a huge pool of small investments. There are thousands of them available, covering every imaginable form of investment.
- Some of these funds are actively managed. You are paying for a company (or a person) to pick investments based on some sort of cunning strategy.
- The really big ones are passively managed and are just buckets of big groups of shares, like every big company in the United Kingdom (the FTSE) or every big company in the world.[10]
- Most people should just buy these funds. That's it. The end.

Look at the chart in Figure 10.1 showing UK house prices and the US stock market over the last 50 or so years. Prices go up and down, sometimes very dramatically, but over the long term the trend is up very significantly. So, if you buy a house, or shares, don't get too stressed if the value moves about a bit – over the long term you should expect to have a nice increase in the value of your investment.

---

[8] Of course, someone decided to give shares lots of other names to make it more confusing for us: shares are also called equities, stocks or securities. Let's just stick with shares.
[9] Makes eating an M&S prawn sandwich even more enjoyable.
[10] As of December 2024, the three biggest funds, in this case Exchange Traded Funds (ETFs), are all over half a trillion dollars. They all track the S&P 500, the biggest companies in the US, and all have very low fees.

Figure 10.1 Shares versus Property

The smartest financial person I know[11] has 100% of his pension and long-term investments in three huge funds. Warren Buffet, widely regarded as the greatest investor of all time, said: 'In my view, for most people, the best thing to do is own the S&P 500 index fund ... The trick is not to pick the right company. The trick is to essentially buy all the big companies through the S&P 500[12] and to do it consistently and to do it in a very, very low-cost way.' So do that.[13] Over the past 20 years, this would have made you an average return of 11.3%. Even better, since it's an index fund, there are no active managers to pay. This may seem like a trivial point but it's an important one. The fees on funds can seriously erode your returns especially when

---

[11] This was his edit of the document.
[12] This is an index of all the big US companies; he is a Yank after all.
[13] Unless you know better, if which case hats off. Looking forward to seeing you in the global rich list above Warren (currently #3 as of November 2024). Never heard of him? He isn't flashy, I suspect he is an ODT under the MSPI ranking.

10 THINGS I ~~HATE~~ LOVE ABOUT MONEY

calculated over a long period of time. There are some excellent books written about this phenomenon including the aptly titled *Where Are the Customers' Yachts?*, written by Fred Schwed Jr. The premise of the title is a man visits New York City and admires the yachts of all the bankers and brokers. He then asked where all the customers' yachts were, those people who followed the advice of these bankers and brokers. The relevant point is that the finance industry isn't always looking out for your best interests, and this is proven daily in the world of funds, with their fee structures.

WHICH INVESTMENT FOR WHICH TIME FRAME?

So, let's do it:

1. **Short term**. A normal bank account is your best bet; even though they often pay little or no interest, there are often lots of cashback and offers, and the best ones have tons of features to help you spend well.[14] This far outweighs a little bit of interest over a couple of months for all the reasons we have discussed in this book.
2. **Medium term**: Put your money in a high-interest savings account (because it doesn't go up and down in value). There are plenty of them out there, there are even great services which will allow you to access lots of them.[15] You can find the best rates with a simple web search.[16]
3. **Long term**: If you want a house, have enough money for the deposit, and can afford it, do it. Put the rest into big shares through low-fee tracker funds. Do this through ISAs and pensions.[17]

---

[14] If I may recommend HyperJar. Again.
[15] Examples: Raisin and Flagstone.
[16] I'm going to recommend Money Saving Expert again. It's a great site.
[17] If you have enough money to fully invest your pension and your £20,000 ISA allowance bravo! You are definitely part of the 1%. Personally, I would just continue to buy funds and pay the tax on it.

And that is it. You are done. I'm going to go into a little more detail on a few relevant topics below, how to get set up, debunk a few myths. But I want to just pause here and point out how simple this actually is. Simple right? Let's crack on.

FOUR PRINCIPLES

Just like spending, successful saving and investing comes down to a few simple rules that are easy to execute. There's no point in having a sophisticated complex strategy that is so overwhelming to put in place and maintain that you don't actually do it.

1. **You just have to start.** Just like going to the gym for the first time, going for your first run, and obviously starting to manage your spending (hooray), one of the first things you must do to get a grip on investing is to simply start. It seems intimidating but it isn't. Don't leave it until you have loads of money, don't think it's something you do in 10 years' time. Even just investing tiny amounts will help you understand what is going on. And those tiny amounts will add up alongside building a habit and your investing muscles.
2. **Small amounts are just fine.** A big part of becoming a successful saver and investor is discovering the wonderful sensation that saving makes you feel (it's bloody great). It's not about slotting away massive amounts once in a blue moon. Not only are regular savings and investments a shortcut to lots of financial dopamine, it also makes sense for shares, in so far as you remove some market risk by investing on lots of different days rather than putting down a big lump once a year.
3. **Think about access to your money.** Money saved in high interest rate accounts or invested in ISAs is easy to access if you need it. You don't even need to smash your cherished porcelain piggy

bank (one advantage of the digital economy). Money invested in your home, or a pension is much more difficult to access – it really is put away for the long term. Is this a good or a bad thing? It certainly poses an interesting question: ISA versus Pension? We will discuss this below.

4. **Simplicity is the superpower**. Just like spending principles, saving follows the 80/20 rule. You can make it infinitely complex[18] if you want to; but for most people you will get everything you could possibly want and need by doing a few key simple things well.

WHY DIFFERENT TIME FRAMES REQUIRE DIFFERENT STRATEGIES

Look at the chart in Figure 10.2:

- Assuming you started investing in any given month over the last 50 years, the tables show you the distributions of returns you would have achieved on cash, shares and property if you left your money invested for 1, 5, 10 and 25 years respectively.
- Let's look at the first box. This is saying that over 1 year, you would have made *on average* 13.2% on houses, 12.6% on shares, and 6% on cash. However, you *might have lost* 11.8% on houses and 41.2% on shares. Compare this to cash where you can't lose money. The percentages below show the probability of getting a return in the range showed on the right. For example: in 23% of cases, one would have made between 10 and 15% on houses.

---

[18] Many investment firms, advisors and hedge funds do this.

Rule 10: Begin Saving and Investing Daily

- Now let's look at the long term. Over 25 years you would have got *average* returns of 12.3% on houses, 10.6% on shares and 5.8% on cash. The *least* you would have got is 9.6%, 7.3% and 2.4% respectively. So, based on the lived in experience of the last 50 years, for a long investment time frame you can deduce that houses and shares have historically been a better idea than cash.

Figure 10.2 Investment Returns over Different Time Frames

		1 Year			5 Years			10 Years			25 Years		
		House	Shares	Cash	House	Shares	Cash	House	Shares	Cash	House	Shares	Cash
	Mean	13.2%	12.6%	6.0%	12.5%	11.9%	6.0%	12.3%	11.5%	5.9%	12.3%	10.6%	5.8%
	Minimum	-11.8%	-41.2%	0.1%	1.7%	-5.9%	0.4%	5.5%	-3.6%	0.4%	9.6%	7.3%	2.4%
	Maximum	42.2%	60.4%	16.7%	25.5%	30.0%	13.1%	22.7%	19.4%	11.7%	16.8%	16.8%	9.9%
From	To												
-50%	-45%												
-45%	-40%												
-40%	-35%		1%										
-35%	-30%												
-30%	-25%		1%										
-25%	-20%		1%										
-20%	-15%		3%										
-15%	-10%	1%	3%										
-10%	-5%	1%	5%										
-5%	0%	1%	6%			10%			5%				
0%	5%	15%	8%	42%	8%	9%	46%		6%	40%			38%
5%	10%	22%	11%	30%	38%	12%	21%	36%	24%	33%	11%	53%	62%
10%	15%	23%	15%	25%	9%	34%	33%	30%	36%	27%	65%	42%	
15%	20%	20%	15%	2%	28%	22%		24%	28%		25%	4%	
20%	25%	7%	11%		15%	8%		10%					
25%	30%	3%	9%		2%	4%							
30%	35%	2%	6%										
35%	40%	4%	4%										
40%	45%	1%	1%										
45%	50%		1%										
50%	55%												

Basically, this can be summarised as follows:

- If your saving time frame is over 10 years – go for it; it's not without risks but buying houses and shares is generally considered the best plan.
- If you expect to spend your money in 5–10 years' time you might start moving some money from shares into cash, so you know exactly what you have got for planning purposes.
- Inside of five years, if you need certainty on your funds (for example, for retirement) then it's probably a good idea to be mainly in cash. The incremental return you might get from being invested in shares for a few years may not be worth the risk that you have a few bad years.
- Pretty much all general investing advice says the same thing: over the longer term take more risk, as you approach retirement, move into less risky investments.[19]
- Property is an interesting one – clearly the vast majority of people who own a house continue to do so for many years – so it is both a phenomenal long-term investment, it isn't that volatile (short drops tend to work themselves out very quickly as you can see in the five-year chart), its hugely tax efficient, and you get to live in it. The flipside is that, because you live in it, most people don't consider it to be an investment. This is clearly not true, in the long term: for downsizing; for paying for care; for leaving something to the children, houses can be wonderful investments, and in the short to medium term, it can do wonders for your DON.[20]

---

[19] They will often talk about bonds and bond funds. Controversially, I'm not so sure, I'll talk about it later on.

[20] Houses: I used a combination of the House Price Index combined with estimates of rental yield. Shares: I used my old favourite the S&P 500 (the biggest US companies – therefore basically the biggest companies) assumed reinvestment and added in adjustments for the exchange rate. Cash: I simply compounded the UK Bank of England base rate as a proxy.

ISAs, PENSIONS AND TAX

So, if it's all about cash, houses and shares what is all this stuff with ISAs and pensions about then? It's all about tax.

Benjamin Franklin famously said, 'In this world nothing can be said to be certain, except death and taxes'. Taxes is everyone's favourite subject, right? Why are taxes in an investing section? Because it's one of the most important factors in ensuring you keep as much of your hard-earned money as possible rather than sending it to the government.

Tax laws in the United Kingdom are extremely complicated. The UK tax code is 10 million words, or 21,000 pages long. As of 2009 when the UK tax code reached 11,520 pages, it was officially the longest in the world. The conclusion of this[21] is I don't expect anyone to be an expert on tax and you don't need to be:

- Just be aware of a few key points set out below.
- The rest is just noise that you don't need to worry about.
- The government is basically on your side, as they want to encourage you to save.
- If you are a normal person with a relatively normal investing plan you shouldn't really be paying any tax on gains at all.

Here are four significant areas the government has covered to encourage savings (more personal savings means less support the government needs to provide for retirees, which is especially helpful):

Cash in the bank:
- Cash is boring, so boring that we almost ignore it. It has been so boring for so long that we don't even think about it as an investment tool. For an unusual period of time, from around 2008 until 2023,

---

[21] Apart from it clearly being utterly ridiculous and in desperate need of reform.

10 THINGS I ~~HATE~~ LOVE ABOUT MONEY

most people didn't even think about savings accounts and interest rates because they were always close to zero. Only in the past year or so have interest rates risen so now savings accounts matter again.
- If you're a lower rate taxpayer, you can earn up to £1,000 of interest on cash in the bank without paying tax on it.[22]
- Higher rate taxpayers can earn £500 tax free.
- Additional rate taxpayers it is £0. Consider putting cash in ISAs.
- Up to £85,000 in a single bank is guaranteed by the government.[23]

Individual Savings Account (ISA):
- You can put cash, funds, shares and bonds in an ISA. An ISA is just a tax 'wrapper' which sits around other investments. The words some people use to describe ISAs get really confusing, talk about 'buying an ISA', or 'using your ISA allowance' when it's really just a type of account which you can put cash and shares in. They are incredibly easy and cheap to set up, you just call one of the many companies who can provide you with one.[24]
- You can put in up to £20,000 per year which, when you think about it for a minute, is a hell of lot. Do that every year you will have a very happy retirement indeed.
- You never pay any tax on any interest or capital gains.
- You can remove your money at any point in time without any penalty, but you don't get your allowance back.

---

[22] It takes a lot of money saved to earn £1,000 of interest.
[23] Through something called the FSCS guarantee scheme. Banks boast about being FSCS guaranteed, which is somewhat ironic given the scheme is there to protect consumers from banks blowing up like they did in the Great Financial Crisis. It's a bit like me boasting that I'm wearing nappies when I come round your house, so I don't mess up your carpet. Frankly if you have more than £85 K in cash then I would suggest that you might want to think about investing in something more interesting than cash.
[24] Some people have lots of different ISAs with lots of different providers. This can become a total nightmare to manage. I recommend having a single ISA account with one of the big providers where you can simply invest in (and change your investments in) any fund you like. If you are in the fortunate position to have lots of ISAs already, it's very easy to move them all to a single provider.

- There are five types of ISAs which I'll briefly describe:
  - Stocks and Shares ISA – this allows you to invest in shares or funds. This is the most important sort of ISA for most people. You can use this to buy the funds I was talking about above.
  - Cash ISA – this is just a savings account. If for some reason you are paying interest on your normal savings, consider this, especially if you aren't using up your entire allowance. If you are approaching retirement, you can move money from your Stocks and Shares ISA into a Cash ISA if you need more certainty of exactly how much you have.
  - Lifetime ISA – Only applicable to people between the ages of 18 and 50. It is primarily designed to help you buy your first home or save for later life. You can put up to £4,000 per year in until you are 50. Your first payment in has to occur before you turn 40. This limit is NOT in addition to your overall £20,000 annual limit. This can be in cash or shares. Every year, the government will add a 25% bonus to the amount you put in. This is free money so definitely take it if you can. You can withdraw this money if you're:
    - Buying your first home.
    - Aged 60 or over.
    - Terminally ill with less than 12 months to live.

    If you withdraw for any other reason, you'll pay a 25% withdrawal charge in order for the government to recover their bonus.
  - Junior ISA – this isn't really a different ISA; it simply allows an adult to open an ISA on behalf of their child. Junior ISAs act the same as regular ISAs but have an annual limit of £9,000 per child. This is a great way to start saving for your child's retirement or even education. More importantly, it's a great way to teach children about investing.

- Innovative Finance ISA – this is a bit of an odd one (in my opinion) but it allows you to invest in a peer-to-peer (P2P) network effectively as a lender, earning a higher rate of interest tax free. This will have higher returns but also carry higher risks as the people may not pay back the money.[25]

Pensions:
- There are really three main types of pensions:
    - **The state pension.** We all get this, based on how much National Insurance we have paid. It is worth checking.[26]
    - **Workplace pensions.** Arranged by your employer. They are either: defined benefit, where you get a guaranteed income based on your salary and how long you have worked there; or defined contribution, where your employer puts money in a pot, and it gets invested in funds (like an ISA or a SIPP, see below). Often you can put more money into your workplace defined contribution scheme.
    - **Personal pensions.** Ones you arrange yourself – either a Stakeholder or a Self-Invested Personal Pension Plan (SIPP).
- For some reason the rules about how you can and cannot invest in pensions are really complex and change all the time. Basically, pensions are often used as a political football by subsequent governments, which makes them unnecessarily complex and somewhat frustrating to understand.
- The main advantage of a (defined contribution) pension scheme is you can put money that you earn in pre-tax. So, for example: if you are a 40% higher rate taxpayer, and you put £12K into a pension you effectively get an extra £8K added to your pot.

---

[25] I don't recommend this. Some silly political nonsense. P2P lenders used to be all the rage – a long time ago. It just makes the whole ISA proposition more confusing. Ah the twists and turns of financial fashion.
[26] You can do this on the gov.uk website.

Rule 10: Begin Saving and Investing Daily

- The downside of a pension is, unlike an ISA, you have to pay tax when you take money out of it in retirement[27] (it is like income).
- There are various reliefs and limits surrounding exactly how much you can put into a pension, especially if you are a very high earner. I'm not going to go into detail here, since the rules change so often that it will probably be out of date before you read it – it's all online – and it is one area where, if you find it remotely confusing – I do actually recommend you getting some advice, however our good old 80/20 rule stands here – you can ignore most of the noise.
- In summary:
  - Make sure your state pension is solid by making sure your NI contributions are up to date.
  - If your employer provides you with a defined benefit pension keep it. It's almost certainly a very good deal.[28]
  - If your employer offers you a defined contribution pension – take it. They often allow you to top it up, often by salary sacrifice. If you can afford to do this, it's almost certainly a good idea to do so.
  - If you have more money to invest over a long time frame you have a choice between ISAs and SIPPs. Because of the pre-tax gross ups, pensions are slightly better mathematically – you will get a little more money when you finally get to spend it but are less flexible if you need the money sooner, since you can't take your money out until you are 55.[29] Lots of people like to debate which is better. The good news is that they are both pretty great ways to invest and get most of your growth tax free, and they will both get you to a good place.

---

[27] You do get to take 25% of it tax free.
[28] Which is why fewer and fewer employers offer them (the government being one of them).
[29] Rising to 57 from 2028. More annoying rules.

10 THINGS I ~~HATE~~ LOVE ABOUT MONEY

Property:
- When you sell your main home, you don't have to pay tax on any sale proceeds. Homes have historically gone up in value, especially over the long term so these gains are completely tax free. If you downsize for example, you can take out a tax-free lump of cash.[30] By the way, there are other ways to take value out of your house when you are older while still living there, such as Lifetime Mortgages.[31]

To summarise on tax:
- Unless you have lots of money then you shouldn't really be paying any tax on investments.[32]
- ISAs, pensions, and property capital gains relief are simply government designed methods to encourage you to invest without paying tax.

EXTERNAL ADVICE

If all this scares you, get some advice. Of course you can do it yourself, just like you can go to the gym yourself, but if you need help and motivation to get going, there are lots of people who can help you – and there is a huge amount of great information online. Paying for a bit of advice and getting going is far better than doing nothing at all – same as getting a personal trainer. In my view there are two kinds of advice:

- Advice in getting stuff set up.
- Ongoing advice on investing.

---

[30] Then consider investing this into cash or shares.
[31] You definitely need to get advice on these however: https://www.equityreleasecouncil.com/
[32] And if you do, and you have blown through your ISA and pension limits well done. And well done for paying more tax.

The former I'm a fan of, the latter I'm not. There are an awful lot of people who pay an awful lot of money for advice which is basically: buy big funds with shares in.

Advisors can come in handy in setting up the following stuff:

- A mortgage broker to help you with getting a mortgage. Ensure you don't pay any extra fees and that they are paid for by the lender. Ask this upfront and if the broker does have a fee, tell them you'll find someone else, and I can promise you they'll drop the fee.
- An accountant to ensure you're getting all the tax breaks available to you. This is especially important if you have a small business.
- A lawyer to help set you up a will.
- A financial advisor to sort out all your pensions. Lots of people, especially those who have had many different jobs, have bits of pension investments in many different places. It really is worth trying to consolidate them all. There are people who have lots of experience in this and its fiddly.

That's what I recommend. Feel free to get advice beyond this but don't feel like you need to. You can honestly do most of this on your own.

As far as advice on investing? Unfortunately, the financial industry has plenty of ways conflicts of interest can appear. I have a friend in Canada whose father was repeatedly given bad advice from a wealth manager who worked for one of the large reputable banks. The manager kept on recommending penny stocks which earned him an incredible commission – he would have made very little if he had provided the simple advice, put it in a fund.

Advisors can earn more fees for doing more complex investments and doing more 'stuff'. An ethical advisor will attempt to avoid these conflicts, but unfortunately not everyone acts ethically.

PAYING OFF DEBT

Of course, one action you should take before you get too excited about investing is to think about your debts. With the honourable exception of a mortgage, almost all personal debt is going to have an interest rate on it higher than you can probably achieve with your investments so it's a good idea to start to pay it off as a first step.

Even consider paying your mortgage down. Can you get more interest investing in shares than your mortgage costs you? Probably over the long term. But paying off your mortgage feels great, and you would be surprised how fast the time to final payment changes with relatively modest overpayments.

Table 10.1 shows how a mortgage[33] maturity changes with overpayments.

So paying an extra 10% on your mortgage payment each year can reduce a 25-year mortgage by almost 5 years. I'm not suggesting that everyone can do this, but as people get older a combination of (hopefully) rising income, and the effects of inflation usually make mortgages become more affordable over time.

Table 10.1 Accelerate Loan Maturity by Overpayments

Remaining Years:		25	20	15	10	5
		\multicolumn{5}{c}{New Remaining Years}
Overpayment	5%	22.5	18.3	13.9	9.4	4.7
	10%	20.5	16.9	12.9	8.8	4.5
	25%	16.3	13.7	10.8	7.5	3.9
	50%	12.3	10.5	8.4	6.0	3.2
	75%	9.9	8.6	6.9	5.0	2.7
	100%	8.3	7.2	5.9	4.3	2.3

---

[33] Assuming a 6% interest rate and a repayment mortgage.

OTHER STUFF PEOPLE INVEST IN

Before we wrap up, and in the same spirit as the bulk of the book, understanding what other people invest in, or will encourage you to invest in, can be helpful either in avoiding certain investments or making sure you go in with your eyes wide open. The following is a (very) non-exhaustive list of investments that advisors, or people down the pub, like to talk about.

Bonds

Bonds are also known as notes, fixed income securities, debentures or credit.[34] This is when you become a lender to a company or the government. Businesses and governments are always borrowing money. They sometimes borrow this money from banks, but they often borrow this money from regular people like you.[35] When you lend to a company, you do it in the form of a bond or loan. That company will pay you interest to account for the risk that they may go bankrupt and also the missed opportunity to earn interest in your bank account. So, for example, as of December 2024 our old friends Marks & Spencer have the following bonds outstanding:

- 4.75% due June 2025
- 3.75% due May 2026
- 3.25% due July 2027
- 7.125% due 2037

Why do they all have different interest rates? Well, they were all issued at different times in the past and they all mature at different times. This

---

[34] Lots more terminology to make people sound clever, it's all the same.
[35] I know you're not regular, I know you're special. Yes you. I was just using a figure of speech, so the not so special people (not you) also felt included.

10 THINGS I ~~HATE~~ LOVE ABOUT MONEY

means as interest rates move, the price you can buy or sell a bond moves (generally interest rates go up, all bond prices go down and vice versa).

This may sound risky, lending money to a company that might become bankrupt, but it's less risky than equity. This is because of how bankruptcy works. If a company goes bankrupt, experts have to step in to try to pay back all the company liabilities using whatever money is left. There's an order of priority and bondholders rank above shareholders.

Of course, the riskier the bond, the higher the rate of interest you will expect to be paid. For example: the least risky bonds[36] in the United Kingdom are issued by the government and are called Gilts, so they will always have the lowest effective rate, and then rates go up from there.

Just like shares, you can invest in individual bonds, but outside of buying Gilts[37] very few individuals buy bonds; people tend to invest in big funds containing lots of bonds (just like funds containing lots of shares). Lots of people do this, especially as they approach retirement, since bond funds seem less risky than shares and should earn you more interest than simply putting your cash in the bank. Nice idea.

The only problem is that, as explained above, the value of bonds and therefore many entire bond funds go up and down as interest rates go down and up. So, lots of people saw the value of their bond fund investments drop pretty dramatically over the last few years as interest rates shot up. Now lots of people (who probably sell bond funds) will probably tell you not to worry, when interest rates go down, the value of bond funds will shoot up again. Will they? Are you an expert on predicting interest rates? I've been working in the bond markets for most of my life and I haven't got a clue.

Bond funds aren't a bad idea, and if you have money invested in bonds, good for you, but in my opinion, and this will probably be the most controversial statement I'm making in the book, for most normal people the

---

[36] In theory.
[37] And there are some very good reasons to do this for certain people, but that's beyond the scope of this book.

increased return over cash in the short to medium isn't worth the risk of prices going up and down, and over the long term you are better off in shares. So don't bother unless you really know what you are doing.

Foreign Currencies

Some people invest in foreign currencies. There are traders who build careers trading currencies. Do you have a view on how sterling is going to change versus the euro or the dollar? No? Then don't do it. The only reason you should hold other currencies is if you have known future expenses (such as a holiday) in another country and you want to lock the rate in now to *lower* your uncertainty – the total opposite of what the traders are doing.

Spread Betting

The clue is in the name. Don't go there. There are all kinds of exotic trading strategies available in dedicated apps which are essentially betting and gambling under the cover of the name 'trading'. Some of these sites are very well done and very popular.[38] It is perfectly possible to make money trading, just like an absolute expert can make consistent money betting on the horses, but most traders who make money work for specialist companies with vast financial resources and huge amounts of information. I doubt this is you.

This is the point where I'm meant to say, spread betting, gambling, trading can be fun, and you should do it if you like, but it should not form the basis of any part of your investing strategy. Well, the latter is certainly true, but about it being fun? I'm going to be a grumpy old man here. Really? Take a long hard look at your money (before you probably lose it) and think of all the other cool things you could do with it.

---

[38] For example: eToro.

Cryptocurrencies

Increasingly popular, for cryptocurrencies look no further than bitcoin – which you could argue is a form of currency or an investible asset like gold. I don't want to upset any crypto bros reading this, but I view crypto in its present state as basically gambling, and regardless of your views, it's always represented as a USD value, so it's hardly a currency in its own right.[39] Regardless of this debate, the price swings in cryptocurrencies are wild – back to our basic principles, you might think this would be OK over the very long term, if you could take a view that the price, like shares, would broadly go up over time. Taking a view on where bitcoin will be, or even if it will be a thing, in 20 years' time is a very deep conversation indeed and it is highly debated. Are you qualified to take a view?

Gold and Commodities

Speaking of currency, we also have gold and commodities. Many people consider these to be investment assets and, in many ways, they are; you can buy them neat, or you can buy them in various forms of fund. Precious metals include gold, silver and platinum, plus more exotic elements like palladium and rhodium.[40] Commodities include crude oil, soybeans, wheat and pork belly futures.[41]

Fortunes are made and lost trading commodities so it's good to be aware of them. Many people like to buy them because they are sometimes seen as uncorrelated with shares, when markets crash quite often metals and commodities don't, and they sometimes go up. Lots of people who talk about investments talk about correlation and 'balancing a portfolio'. In my

---

[39] No one would care about a bitcoin if you couldn't convert it into a real currency like dollars or pounds.
[40] As a geek I find these rare elements rather exciting. Don't ever let that get in the way of making the right investment decisions though!
[41] Pork belly futures were famously depicted in the 1980s classic movie *Trading Places* starring Eddie Murphy and Dan Akroyd.

view, for long-term investing, a hugely diversified portfolio of shares is just fine; if there is a sufficiently large lack of correlation in the underlying portfolio it doesn't need to be made more complex by investing in gold and commodities, however cool. But don't let me stop you – these are perfectly valid investments (and quite cool).

Wine and Farms

Certain investments have, for slightly mysterious reasons, interesting tax advantages. For example:

- You don't have to pay capital gains tax on wine.[42]
- Until recently you didn't have to pay inheritance tax on farmland.[43]

These crazy investments, and I include cars and art in this, are a sport for very rich people who have long gone past the obvious tax-free allowances in pensions and ISAs. I bring them up here to make a serious point: lots of unusual investments are fads.

Wine investment was all the rage for many years, partly because prices were driven up by a huge surge in drinking expensive booze by the Chinese. Now they have got bored of it, and fine wine prices are in the doldrums. I know a few people who are genuine experts in this space, who actually made a reasonable amount of money, and now wouldn't touch it with a bargepole.

Be aware of the 'new thing' in investing, there is always some kind of get-rich-quick scheme or idea that people are giddy about; trust me, they are simply not worth thinking about unless you are an absolute expert – which you're not, so we're not going to think about them.

---

[42] And you can drink it.
[43] It is still advantageous from a tax point of view, but the overall exemption was removed at the end of 2024 much to the anger of many farmers. And many rich people who bought farms mainly because of the tax breaks. I love Jeremy Clarkson – have you watched *Clarkson's Farm*? I recommend it.

10 THINGS I ~~HATE~~ LOVE ABOUT MONEY

I know dozens of very successful people who are very financially sophisticated with plenty of savings who never venture outside of cash, shares, houses and to be fair bonds – let's call them the big four (and you know I'm going to recommend you stick to the even bigger three). Never, literally never. If you are investing in anything apart from the big four and you haven't got pots of money (and lots of your pots of money invested in the big four) then you are quite possibly bonkers, and I don't want to talk to you since you aren't listening.[44]

I'm going to go even further – except for entertainment and learning – don't even bother to invest in a share or a bond of a single company aside from one exception: which is to learn using a tiny amount of money.

I read an article in a major English newspaper this morning trying to explain 'price earnings ratio' for shares. No. Just no. Don't even think about trying to work this nonsense out.

Just put your money in a few diversified funds. You don't need to understand shares at all or even a company's business prospects. Let someone else do all the work. We're going to leverage statistics, diversification, low fees and leave it at that.

PUTTING IT ALL TOGETHER

What follows is an action plan that will work for the vast majority of people.

1. Have a single account for your day-to-day spending. Preferably one that is free, which has nice offers attached, and has the ability to divide your money up into sub-accounts[45] to make managing your spending easier.

---

[44] Okay fine, you just read this and didn't have a chance to rectify your situation, so I'll still talk to you.
[45] Jars / pots / vaults / spaces / envelopes.

Rule 10: Begin Saving and Investing Daily

2. Open a nice high interest account to keep your rainy-day fund, your sunny-day fund and any amounts of money you know you aren't going to spend in the next 3–6 months.
3. Find a single provider to set up your investment accounts. This will allow you to do all of your ISAs, any personal pensions, any other investments in one place. The big providers[46] all offer a complete service and are reputable, but each has advantages and disadvantages based on your circumstances. There are loads of reviews online. Personally, I would stay away from providers who sell their own funds, but that is just me.
4. Start putting some funds into your savings and investment accounts today. This is the most important step. If you have established your DON and have some regular excess, try to move some money across regularly. Start small. Too many people feel they aren't ready or need to wait or need more money. You don't. The most important thing is to get started immediately.
5. If you have a workplace pension sign up for it, if you can do salary sacrifice into your pension do it. Out of sight, out of mind.
6. Pay off any debts apart from your mortgage.
7. Fill up your rainy-day fund with 3–6 months of essential expenses.
8. Start putting some money in your sunny-day fund but invest money while you are doing this.
9. Use your ISA allowance and begin by buying into a stocks and shares ISA. Buy an Exchange Traded Fund (ETF) with low management fees. Start with a global tracker, something that invests in stocks and shares from around the world.
10. If you manage to use up your entire ISA allowance, or you don't have a workplace pension scheme, consider starting a SIPP pension and put your long-term investment money in there.

---

[46] Some of the biggest: Hargreaves Lansdown, AJ Bell, Interactive Investor, Fidelity International, Vanguard.

11. Try to automate this investing. Transfer money over regularly. It's fun. You can look at your phone every day and see how much you have got and how much it's worth.
12. Review your portfolio monthly. You can consider changing things as you become more comfortable with the process.
13. If you have children and you give them pocket money, consider forcing half or more of it into a Junior ISA. You will build for their future and teach them about savings. The other half can be used for spending, or they can choose to invest it as well. If you come across a bonus or extra money, you should consider trying to maximise your ISAs, both for yourself and your kids.

That's it, that's the Action Plan. Easier than you thought, wasn't it?

It's very simple. The most important thing is to get started today. If you do that, that will be more powerful than any kind of sophisticated strategy.

RULE 10 WRAP-UP

This rule is about how we are going to reap the rewards of good spending habits by turning any excess money into enduring wealth and peace of mind.

- Investing is actually really simple (once you ignore the staggering amounts of noise).
- Most people who know what they are doing, do pretty much exactly the same thing. Do what they do.
- It takes a little bit of work to set yourself up to invest, but it's not very hard, and you only have to do it once.
- Investing strategy – what you are going to do – and investing – actually doing it – are separate. Most people don't get this. You only need to think about investing strategy once in a blue moon, you should invest whenever you can.

- Begin investing today, little and often is much better than big and infrequent.
- Investing is fun, seeing your savings increase is great, and seeing them grow whilst you are down the pub is even better.
- You don't need to use a professional advisor to get the basics down. Most people can do this on their own. But if you do feel you need the help of a professional advisor you absolutely should. They are many excellent professionals who know what they are talking about and can get you started. However, think carefully about ongoing fees for ongoing investment management or advice once you are set up.

CHAPTER ELEVEN

BONUS RULE 11: PARENT GUIDE FOR HELPING YOUR KIDS

As a parent you have the ability to put your child on a path to money mastery, even if you aren't a master yourself.

'They fuck you up, your mum and dad.
They may not mean to, but they do.
They fill you with the faults they had
And add some extra, just for you.'
—*Philip Larkin, 'This Be the Verse'*

'Giving children pocket money is not just about generosity; it's about teaching responsibility.'
—*Richard Branson*

What I hate – Children need their nappies changed, and bloody hell do they ever reduce your DON something rotten.

What I love – You can teach your kids about finance and help them have a really happy life (even if you didn't know a thing prior to reading this book and then as a bonus they will have the means to look after you if you ever need your nappies changing).

What is the best way to get your kids in shape? It is to lead by example. And if you lead by example, as a bonus, you are going to be getting in shape yourself.

Kids aren't stupid, they pay more attention to what parents do than what they say. If you're telling your kids to eat healthy food and get out and play sports but meanwhile, you're eating at McDonald's and watching Netflix, your kids will know you're a hypocrite before they even know the meaning of the word. On the other hand, if you're making healthy meals, going outside and being active and making fitness fun, your kids are more likely to take that habit with them.[1]

You don't need to be an expert. Try and do the right thing rather than saying the right thing. Put yourself out there, make the odd mistake but bounce back and try again.

So, let's turn back to money and kids.

THE THREE BEARS

I think it's appropriate in a section on children to use a fairy tale as a section header don't you?

---

[1] One day. Maybe there will be a painful decade of rebellion first, but one day they will. I hope.

In my family, the problem with financial education is getting the temperature just right. My father cooked the financial porridge too cold; I have often cooked it too hot.

As I mentioned at the beginning of the book, my parents were very frugal with money but steady providers of all our needs. We had an excellent balance of hand-me-down toys and clothes and exciting new presents at Christmas and birthdays. However, we were given an allowance[2] but we simply weren't allowed to spend it. It sat in a savings account accumulating interest. This was in the 1980s when interest was extremely high, so the growth was meaningful. I remember dad getting furious about almost any spending we did; our pocket money was just for saving up. I remember my sister Jackie being grounded for buying a small cactus plant. I remember buying a car magazine[3] in secret; when I was found out it was as if I had been buying Class A drugs considering the telling off that I was given.

The reality was that my parents were so strict about money that we learned absolutely nothing about spending well because we weren't allowed to spend at all.[4] Is it surprising that I went off the rails a little when I got my first paycheque?[5]

I also think my upbringing has impacted my relationship with my own children.[6] I'm a single father of four and my kids are the most important thing in my life.

---

[2] The Canadian equivalent to pocket money.
[3] It had a picture of a Ferrari on it – it blew my 12-year-old mind.
[4] It's a bit like kids getting into smoking and drinking precisely because their parents tell them not to. There is quite a lot of literature on why adults in certain countries (like France and Italy) have a more healthy relationship with alcohol than other countries (like the United Kingdom) because they were allowed to drink a little as children at dinner.
[5] When I was 25, I suddenly made close to half a million US dollars. This was an enormous sum. Because I had lived such a frugal life up until then, I didn't know what to do with myself. I never experienced this sense of ease, so I went nuts buying stuff. I detailed my car shopping spree. I did months-long trips to Maui, Cape Hatteras, the Caribbean, heli-skiing in Alaska. I was living the good life. I basically spent it all and I didn't invest. It was fun. I guess I learned the right lessons in the end.
[6] Sorry mum and dad, a lot of this is entirely my own fault, I'm just trying to make a point in a book, OK?

The main mistake I have made is swinging too far in the opposite direction of my parents. I have had more disposable income than my parents had, and I am definitely a more profligate spender. I have a high tolerance for risk compared to my dad and it reveals itself the way I live life. I don't generally worry too much about money; I always have confidence that I'll be able to 'figure something out' when I need to. I've gone through divorce, layoffs, not being paid, having a sick toddler with cancer, founding a startup with no salary for years, being an expat raising children without any help. But I always feel like I'll figure it out. This laissez-faire attitude has extended to how I raise my kids. I pay for lots of things because I want to maximise their opportunities but also have fun. If they feel like going go-karting, we're going go-karting. If I want to wakeboard, we're going to wakeboard and if my kids want to try, the thought isn't 'How will I pay for it?', it's 'How exciting, my kid wants to wakeboard with me'. So, while they have allocated pocket money, I have given them carte blanche to spend as they please, but worse still, I add on trainers, Thorpe Park tickets, a new basketball, mostly what they want. I just buy it. Let's face it – they are spoiled.[7]

I'm not sure who is worse, me or my father. My father wouldn't let us spend at all, I let my children have too much and so I've not done a very good job teaching how to spend well either.

How on earth do you get the porridge just right?

Looking back, I believe the middle way is the right answer:

1. My parents should have let me use some of my pocket money as I pleased. I could choose to buy something useless straight away or save up to buy a Nintendo system. But make me go without if I blew it. Learn some lessons about the short-term joys of consumption out of my system in a more controlled way.

---

[7] Although compared to some of the children of my friends? I don't think so. Try working in central London and see what some teenagers get away with. It's all relative.

2. I shouldn't continuously top-up my kids spending when they use all their pocket money. I need to teach them some of the lessons set out in this book about delayed gratification and DON.
3. My parents were right to teach me and my siblings about investment, but investment without any explanation of why you are doing it and to what end is very hard to understand as a child.
4. I realised I needed to start to teach my children about investment (as well as spending) so started to put money aside for them for the future, but in a visible way that they can see and understand.[8]

I'm not trying to sit here and judge my parents. I think they did an amazing job. But we're going for perfect.

It's far too easy to be overly protective of our kids, I know I do it. In health it's called the Hygiene Hypothesis: we keep our kids from being exposed to germs and mess when they are growing up – they end up with an increased risk of developing allergies. I think it's the same in finance – the Financial Hygiene Hypothesis if you like. So, what is the financial porridge that is just right?

I think the real lesson is that you need to allow your kids to simulate the real world in an environment where they won't get hurt, when they are younger, and to learn lessons that will help them when they are on their own.

LIFE SIMULATION

So, the plan is a life simulation. We're going to create an environment where our kids can learn within a bubble. It's like raising a toddler. Toddlers have the 'terrible twos' because they are mini teenagers trying to exert some independence after being so reliant on mum and dad. We need to let them

---

[8] Children's ISAs are a great tool for this.

play and explore and have their tantrums. But we guide it. We don't just let them crawl around a swimming pool unattended because they'll drown. We let them walk around and fall; we intervene when they can seriously hurt themselves. It's okay if they fall off their bike.[9] I think it's important they learn how to manage risks on their own to a large degree.

When it comes to spending, we need to create the same environment. We are building a life simulation. We give kids autonomy but not full autonomy.

Here's how we do it:

1. **Let them make mistakes**. Give them pocket money that they can choose to spend as they please. I think this makes sense at around eight years old as a guide. A younger child doesn't care about things as much, they just love the ability to buy something occasionally, even if it's an ice cream. When your child reaches secondary school is when you must really give them more freedom to make mistakes.

2. **Teach delayed gratification**. Delayed gratification is a skill in itself that leads to a savings mindset and discourages impulsive spending. There's a famous test called the Stanford Marshmallow Experiment. In it, a child was offered a choice between one immediate marshmallow or two marshmallows it they waited for a period of time, 15 minutes. The children would have to wait in the room with the marshmallow and not eat it to earn the second reward. In follow-up studies years later, the researchers learned that the children who were able to wait longer had statistically better life outcomes as measured by academic test scores, education, fitness and other life measures. There is controversy to these conclusions, but there is no controversy that if a child is able to delay gratification, they will be less susceptible to pressure. To teach delayed gratification there are a

---

[9] In my opinion, some may disagree of course.

Bonus Rule 11: Parent Guide for Helping Your Kids

few simple things we can do with our children. The sooner we start the better. These steps are taken from a blog on the website ThinkPsych (ThinkPsych.com, 2024):

(a) Start small. Make children wait to speak, or cook a meal together so they can understand there's a process before you can eat.

(b) Teach your child to stay calm when they don't get what they want straight away. This one can be hard but being calm and reminding them to be calm and find a distraction will become ingrained.

(c) Verbalise rules – 'Only one show', 'One cookie for pudding'. When your child wants to break the rule, say the rule and they will begin to say it themselves (this works great for four-year-olds).

(d) Remove temptations. Younger children have less self-discipline. Don't test their monk skills and rather remove sources of temptation from their sight. If your teen uses too much social media, you shouldn't be on your phone scrolling endlessly yourself.

(e) Use rewards sparingly. You don't want your child expecting a treat every time they tie their shoes. Positive low-key feedback works great for everyday life and big successes that took time to earn can be celebrated with a bigger celebration.

(f) Have consequences for now or later. If your child chose to play video games and now their homework is due in the morning and they haven't started, make them face the consequences. It's the best way for them to learn and they'll soon realise they need to make better choices.

(g) Help with goals. Working towards something is hard. This book has discussed this extensively for adults. Talk to your kids about your goals and how you are working towards them, including the small things you're doing today. You want them to understand that achieving goals is a process and it requires lots of diligent effort. Get them to write them down.

   (h) Encourage independent play. Kids who get everything they want often results in kids who don't know how to entertain themselves. They need other people to entertain them. Many child psychologists have seen a recent phenomenon where kids are 'play deprived' and gravitate towards technology. Independent play away from screens is healthy for your kid. This can be toys, art, sports, board games, music or anything else your kid fancies that isn't technology or junk food.

3. **Be clear about what you will pay for**, and what their pocket money needs to pay for. Give them a level of pocket money where they will need to make choices. They will need to choose to not buy a Costa snack for the next six weeks if they want to go to Thorpe Park Fright Night. For younger ones, start making them understand how they would need to buy a toy they want on their own. If they buy an ice cream each week, they won't ever be able to afford the Barbie doll. A few cycles of this and they will learn and will start making a choice not to buy the ice cream.

4. **Talk to your kids about money.** Talk about your goals and talk about their goals. Talk about goals for the month ahead. By talking about money, you're going to help them avoid the social mistakes we talked about before and give them confidence to ask questions if they don't know. Too many people worry about looking stupid. You don't want your kids to ever feel that way. It's okay to not know and it's a great thing to ask for help and tuition.

5. **Invest for your children**. But do it though pocket money. Tell them that they are getting a certain amount of pocket money per week. Half of it they get to spend, the other half is going to be saved up for

fun stuff in the future. Let them see it, let them see how fast it starts to add up, let them see the compounding.

POCKET MONEY

Let's quickly talk about pocket money. How much is right and for what ages. For this we can look at averages across the country. There is no hard and fast rule. My advice on how to determine the right amount of pocket money is as follows:

1. Use averages as guidance only but ultimately trust your own instincts. Pocket money for your kids should never impair your ability as a parent to manage your finances and savings goals.
2. Consider what you yourself want to pay for and what you want your kids to cover with pocket money. My advice is to cover more for kids until secondary school, but secondary school provides a lot more autonomy. What are things you may pay for in primary school? Things like trips, eating out with the family, sports kit they need for their sports. Anything special should ideally be reserved for birthdays and Christmas. At secondary school, you start to give them more responsibility. If they want to take the train to their friends, they should build a travel budget. If they want snacks or treats, they can buy that themselves. If they want new trainers or fashionable clothing, they can pay for that. If they want to go bowling or wakeboarding, I think you could contribute. I like encouraging teenagers especially to do fun social activities, so I think it's healthy to subsidise that. But let them contribute as well, perhaps for snacks where they go. It's a very grey area and you need to determine these boundaries for your family situation.

Table 11.1   Average Pocket Money in the UK by Age

Age	Average Pocket Money (£)
4	3.21
5	3.24
6	3.65
7	3.86
8	4.10
9	4.45
10	4.99
11	5.84
12	7.37
13	8.93
14	10.67
15	11.34
16	13.32
17	14.52

Table 11.1 shows average amounts of pocket money per week for children in the United Kingdom. Take this as guidance but do not treat it as gospel. This research was conducted by Finder in 2023.[10]

INVESTING

Why is it so important to teach children about investing? For all the reasons we have discussed in this book of course – but there are a couple of really important points to highlight that particularly affect children:

- Social media, influencers, Tiktok are very fond of some of the more racy backwaters of investing – that is, trading and gambling. A lot of

---

[10] Source: M. Boyle (2023) 'How Much Pocket Money DO Kids in the UK Get?', *Finder*, 11 May, https://www.finder.com/uk/banking/childrens-banking/kids-banking-statistics

very famous, very attractive people with millions of followers are heavily personally invested in cryptocurrencies and promote this stuff relentlessly on social media – and some of the biggest users and consumers of social media are our kids. My eldest daughter and her friends know a great deal about bitcoin and how exciting it is, I doubt more than one of them[11] knows what the S&P 500 is.

- Digital money. We discussed the challenges with the disappearance of cash earlier in the book. For lots of children they are rarely, if ever, going to really see actual coins and notes.

So, what are we going to do about it?

Junior Stocks and Shares ISA

Make this the bread and butter of your child's financial markets education. Set one up as soon as possible, it's easy and costs almost nothing. You don't need to contribute huge amounts – £5 at a time is fine. The key is to contribute regularly and continuously and make it part of the entire pocket money narrative. As soon as you are able to, you want to talk to your child about their Junior ISA. Explain how it works and what's happening. Explain your goals for this.

I recommend investing in the same funds you would for yourself. You can talk about it and enjoy watching your money increase in value together.

More importantly, having a proper investment account, with a meaningful amount of money in it will make putting small amounts of money on risky bets look much less appealing.

Play Money

For very young children, get them play money. Let them count it, play games of shopping. Have them choose to buy things and give you money.

---
[11] My daughter obviously.

It sounds very simple, but you start to embed lessons around scarcity, decision making and simple arithmetic. Often all that is needed is exposure.

Kids Spending Cards

Get your children physical spending cards early to get them more comfortable with digital money. But get one which teaches good spending habits and has great guard rails against really bad spending.[12]

Financial literacy starts with communication and exposure. Letting your child play with money is where it starts. Having open conversations about money is setting them on a path to mastery. This is especially important if you feel insecure about your financial knowledge. There's nothing greater than learning together. You don't need to pretend you're an expert if you're not. Your children will respect you more if you admit areas that you are weak in and where you want to improve. If you do this, I can assure you your children will gain financial literacy.

SPECIFIC PLANS FOR CHILDREN BY AGE

Let's break this down even further by outlining plans for children by age cohort. Clearly these are just guidelines, all kids grow up at different speeds:

So, what can you do legally?

- From birth: parents can setup a Junior ISA as well as, amazingly, a pension.[13]

---

[12] Go on. Take a wild guess at which one I'm going to recommend.
[13] The consumer magazine *Which?*, which I highly recommend, has a great website with a good summary of pension options for children.

- From age 6: pocket money cards such as HyperJar, Rooster and GoHenry, which are e-money accounts with connected contactless debit cards.
- From age 7: savings accounts from high street banks with guardian oversight.
- From age 11: savings accounts and current account with debit card.
- From age 13: Apple Pay and Google Pay (for their pocket money cards).
- From age 16: can setup their own Junior ISA.
- From age 18: pretty much everything including BNPL, credit cards and loans (danger, danger!).

Baby to Early Primary Years (Age 0–6)

Get your kids comfortable with the idea of money. If you're able to, it's also a great time to set up a Junior ISA and give them pocket money (which all goes into the ISA). They may not get it now, but it will be a great thing to talk about over the coming years.

- Pocket money around £2/week.
- Setup a Junior Stocks and Shares ISA to deposit pocket money in directly.
- Buy packs of play money and possibly a cash register.
- Play shop with toddlers and reception age children.
- Talk about how much things cost every time you shop.
- Talk about decisions you make when choosing to buy things or not buy things.
- Talk about saving money and how you have to save to buy nicer things.

Older Primary Years (Age 6–11)

In this phase, they are now old enough to have their own pocket money card and will have a better sense of value. This is when you need to start giving kids autonomy and letting them make their first mistakes and force them to learn how to save up for things they want. This is a phase where as a parent you must be very deliberate in deciding what you will pay for your kids and what their pocket money needs to cover.

- Pocket money from £2–5/week.
- If you don't have a Junior Stocks and Shares ISA set up, set one up now.
- Speak to your child about the ISA and let them help you pick a fund.[14]
- Force a portion of pocket money into the Junior ISA each week.
- Let your kid spend or save any remaining pocket money.
- Encourage them to save up for more expensive items and help them along.
- Get them a pocket money card. Let them start spending using this.
- Allow your child to earn extra money by doing bigger jobs. Give them a connection between work and reward and the ability to work harder and reap the benefits.
- Continue talking about money with your kids. Not just about them but talk to them about your adult situations. Your bills, your goals, your pressures. You don't want to overwhelm them or make them feel scared, but you want to talk confidently about how you organise your money and prioritise things.

---

[14] You already know what this is of course!

Secondary School (Age 11–17)

Besides dealing with teenage rebellion and hormones, now is the time to really help your kids be ready for full financial independence:

- Pocket money from £4–15 – consider making this higher if you want your kids to have to learn to budget and pay for more things themselves (and thus you would pay for less day to day, but the risk is they will run out of money and be left out) – remember to allocated a portion of this to the ISA, no questions, but tell them that they can put more in if they like.[15]
- Get your kids an app which will show them the value of their ISA so they can look at it all the time and gasp.
- Controversially, when they (inevitably) come and talk to you about cryptocurrency or some other nonsense, consider letting them buy a small amount. Back to the thesis of making mistakes, do it now in a controlled way.[16]
- Give them the opportunity to earn extra money through bigger jobs.
- Encourage part-time employment to both earn money and learn to manage their time and priorities.

Higher Education and Young Adulthood (Age 18+)

At this age your kids are on their own, even if you're chipping in with some school tuition. They will be having to run a budget and learn how to pay for their necessities and their entertainment. They will have new friends, roommates and social pressure different from anything they have experienced

---

[15] Consider matching any extra contributions. This works wonders.
[16] And they are probably going to do it anyway with or without your permission.

before. At this stage, hopefully you have instilled some of the lessons before but if not, do not fret, there's still a lot you can do as a parent – buy them this book for their birthday.

RULE 11 WRAP-UP

As a parent or guardian, you have the ability to change your child's future when it comes to money. We know that by being in control of your spending, you reduce anxiety, and you build happiness – give this gift to your children. Teach them that it's not all about wealth, it's about being in control and feeling happy about not squandering your time or money:

1. Start talking about money with kids when they are young. Do this in a happy, objective way, never stressful. Talk about how much things cost, how you earn money, how you have to save for nicer things. Normalise money talk.
2. Have a proper pocket money plan. Let them make mistakes.
3. Set up Junior ISAs for your kids immediately and start investing small amounts into Stocks and Shares ISAs. Get your kids involved, make it part of the pocket money dialogue.
4. Give older kids more autonomy over spending decisions. Let them make mistakes but also let them suffer the consequence if they spend too much and don't save up for bigger events. It might be hard but it's the best way to learn.
5. Teach your kids, no matter their age, the rewards of delayed gratification and help them build skills to ingrain this. This is just as powerful for two-year-olds as it is for adult children who may not have learned this.

CONCLUSION

When it comes to money, it is sometimes very hard to see the wood through the trees due to all of the noise: the financial services industry trying to sell you complex products; the marketing and social media industries trying to encourage you to spend at every turn; lots of complex jargon; your friends and family consciously or subconsciously steering you off the path to financial equilibrium.

If you ignore all the noise, it is very simple: the big message[1] is that getting in control of your money is really all about focusing on spending well.

This is, by many orders of magnitude, the most important action that you can take to improve your financial wellness, and it really isn't difficult to achieve:

- Understand your spending and yourself.
- Realise that lots of small financial actions become very meaningful over time.
- Slow down, pause, take stock.
- Build in everyday good habits starting today.
- If you can, invest a little, and do it often and automatically.

---

[1] In flashing lights and fireworks. I wanted one last footnote.

Do this, and you can turn money into something that you love, not something that you hate.

Even though this book is all about money, money in and of itself doesn't buy happiness, and obsessing over it can lead to an unhappy and unfulfilled life. I can guarantee, however, that understanding and getting on top of your spending, regardless of the absolute amount of money that you have, can have a profound impact on your overall happiness.

I hope you've taken away something from this book that has helped your life, which I hope is long, happy and fulfilling.

If you have any thoughts or ideas after reading this book, please reach out.

Every person I speak to, I learn something new.

Thank you.

ACKNOWLEDGEMENTS

This is the first book I have ever written and the process has been hard but extremely rewarding. I definitely couldn't have done this on my own and have so many people who have provided immense help. First, I want to thank Alice at Wiley who reached out to me in the first place and gave me the confidence to write a book. My HyperJar co-founder Paul who helped plan the book content, challenged and improved my ideas, edited sections, drew pictures and was always generally there when I felt like giving up. My colleague Tricia who is also a friend, for her positive support, helping with editing and sourcing data.[1] My sisters Tonette and Jackie who took time from their busy families and professional lives to edit sections and give valuable feedback. I also want to thank my other co-founder Arthur who gave me the confidence to start HyperJar in the first place but also, as an author, supported me with ideas throughout my writing.

---

[1] I did have to rewrite 30,000 words because of her comments but it was well worth it.

ABOUT THE AUTHOR

Mat Megens is the founder and former chief executive officer of money management app HyperJar. Born on a farm in Canada, he began his career as an electrical engineer and managed to find himself in the thick of the dotcom boom, working with startups in the Boston tech scene. He then made a career change to investment banking in London right around the peak of the credit crisis, including a stint at Lehman Brothers in mortgage trading. This was followed by work in developing economics with the International Finance Corporation (IFC) of the World Bank around the time of the Arab Spring. Looking for a bit more stability, he then founded HyperJar, a fintech, during the crypto and tech boom/bust before and after COVID-19 and the demise of Silicon Valley Bank. Despite this, HyperJar has managed to survive and thrive, and now has almost three quarters of a million customers.

Mat is a single father of four and dedicated to ensuring his children learn great money habits from an early age.

INDEX

A
AA breakdown service   163
acceptance   32–4, 130
access to savings and
    investments   209–10
accountant   219
accounts, multiple   110, 122
Action Plan   226–8
addictions   75–6
Aldi   158, 166, 174
   gift cards   164
Amazon   153, 154, 163, 165,
    169, 175
   gift card   185
Amex cards   165
Android   86, 121
Annual Percentage Rate (APR)   90
anomaly spends   110
Apple   72, 121, 153
   iPhone   86, 171–4
   Pay   243
app subscriptions   73–4
Aristotle   19, 61

artificial intelligence (AI)   172–3
Asda   157
assets   99
auto loans   81
average lifetime earnings (UK)   15

B
bank current accounts   67
bank debt decision calculator   93–7
bank lending flow chart   96
banks   42–3
   high-interest accounts   7 *see also
    under names*
bank statements   109–11
Barclays   67
bargain hunters   159–60
benchmark yourself   114
Best, George   61
bills
   checking   146–7
   splitting   32, 57
binge shopping   38
bitcoin   204, 224

253

INDEX

Blackberry 86
Black Friday 177
BMW 153
bonds 80, 221–3
Boots 162
Boots Advantage 166
borrowers, stopping 194
Branson, Richard 231
breakage 164–5
broad-based discounting (BBD) 162
broken windows theory 71
budgeting 143
  challenges 143
Buffet, Warren 1, 201, 207
bulk buying 168–9
Buy Now Pay Later (BNPL) 6–7, 81, 92, 93, 166, 243

C

CAR (Clueless/Accepting/Reckless) = Nightmare 28, 140, 142
card-linked cashback 162
Carr, Allen 119, 124
cars
  franchised dealerships 154
  repairs 72–3
cash 205, 213–14
cashback 162–3
Cash ISA 215
Casuals 160
CAT (Clueless/Accepting/Thoughtful) = Pleaser 28, 140, 142
CDR (Clueless/Defiant/Reckless) = Ostrich 28, 140
CDT (Clueless/Defiant/Thoughtful) = Hoarder 28, 140, 142
charitable giving 49
children 231–46
  competitiveness and 54
  delayed gratification 236–8
  influence on 55
  investing for 238–9
  investing, teaching about 240–2
  life simulation 235–9
  making mistakes 236
  pocket money 239–40
  saving plans by age 242–6
  saying no 57–8
  talk to, about money 238
  what parent will pay for 238
Citizens Advice 101
Clueless spenders 136, 160, 167
Coca-Cola 153
Colgate 153
commodities 224–5
company gift pools 48
competitiveness 53
compound action 62, 64–71
compound interest 64, 67
Confucius 151
Consumer Price Index (CPI) 167
contract services 167
control, being in 181
Co-operative 67
Costa 68, 238

Index

Costco 169
Cost Per Use (CPU) 130, 144–5, 168
coupons 155
Coveter 29
   changing to IDT 31–3
CPI (Consumer Price Index) 167
credit 221
credit card 81, 82, 93, 95, 110
   child 243
   debt 88–9
cryptocurrencies 224
current account with debit card, children's 243

D

Daily One Number (DON) 118–22
daily saving and investing 201–29
   long-term 205, 208
   medium-term 205, 208
   principles 209–10
   short-term 205, 208
   strategies 210–12
   time frames 205, 208–12
daily spending 3–17
daily surplus 99, 100
dealership associations 155
deals, finding 151–78
debentures 80, 221
debt 79–102
   defined 80–1
   for investment 85
   paying off 220
   reasons for using 84

staying out of 100
traps and spirals 88–90
UK 81–2
debt decision calculator 97–9
defined contribution pension 216, 217
delayed gratification 236–8
delay in spending 169–74
   what we can 170–4
   what we cannot 169–70
Deliveroo 76
Deming, W Edwards 105
Dickens, Charles: *David Copperfield* 3
digital money 241
digital payments, impact of 9–11
direct sales 153
discounts 161–7
discretionary expenses 108, 120
Disney+ 73
disposable economy 72–3
distributors, sales through 153
DON (Daily One Number) 91, 122–4, 139–40
dopamine 33, 70, 129, 136, 184–5
Dopamine Addict 29
double dopamine shopping hit 184–5
drinking rounds 49–50
Dropbox 74

E

earning profiles 59
eBay 175, 177

255

INDEX

Efficient Market Hypothesis 152–3
80/20 rule 14, 175, 210, 217
Einstein, Albert 64
electronics, repairs of 72
Evernote 74
Exchange Traded Fund (ETF) 227
external advice 218–19

F
Facebook, fraudulent sellers on 177
family and friends 45–50
   lending to 47–8, 57
farms 225–6
fashion brands 73
financial advisors 202, 219
Financial Hygiene Hypothesis 235
First Direct 67, 68
fixed income securities 80, 221
food 148
   delivery services 76–7
foreign currencies 223
franchised dealerships 154
Franklin, Benjamin 213
fraud 177
free items 155
Freemium 74
friction in spending 142–3
FSCS guarantee scheme 214
FTSE 206
full price 155–7
funds
   defined 206
   fees on 207–8

future, impact on 183–4
future spending 118–22

G
gambling 204
generosity 58
gift cards 163–5
gift vouchers 162–5
gilts 80, 222
goals 143–4
   long-term 144, 196
   savings 123
   short-term 144
GoHenry 243
gold 224–5
good debt, bad debt 91–2
Google 175
Google Pay 243
Great Financial Crisis 214
group, spending in 57

H
habits 127–49
   bad 130–2
   definition 128–9
   good 132–3
   time taken to form 129–33
happiness 195–7
hermit 29
high-interest bank accounts 7
hire purchase 81
history, spending 105–25
Hoarder 28

Index

Holos kombucha   74
Honey   133, 163, 165, 177–8
Hoover free flights promotion   163
houses   205 *see also* mortgages
HSBC   67
HSBC credit card   165
Hygiene Hypothesis   235
HyperJar   x, xi, 11, 21, 133, 142, 161, 163, 185, 243

I
IAR (Informed/Accepting/Reckless)
   = Coveter   29, 140, 142
   changing to IDT   31–3
IAT (Informed/Accepting/Thoughtful)
   = Hermit   29
IDR (Informed/Defiant/Reckless)
   = Dopamine Addict   29, 140
IDT (Informed/Defiant/Thoughtful)
   = Zen   29, 31–3
impulsiveness   24, 27, 35–7, 130
Individual Savings Account
   (ISA)   205, 213–18
   allowance   227
Individual Voluntary
   Arrangement (IVA)   101
inefficient market theory   152–61
inflation   88, 203
Innovative Finance ISA   216
Instagram   177
interest   67–9
interest rates   88
   on savings accounts   67

investing, defined   203–4
investments   205–8
iPhone   86

J
January sales   177
Jefferson, Thomas   79
John Lewis   153, 165
Junior ISA   215, 228, 242, 243
Junior Stocks and Shares ISA   241

K
Kahneman, Daniel   105
keeping up with the Joneses'   51
Kids Spending Cards   242

L
Larkin, Philip   231
lawyer   219
leverage   85
Levi's   73
Lewis, Martin   159
liabilities   99
Lidl   158, 166
Lifetime ISA   215
Lloyds Bank   177
loans   80
   children   243
long-term saving and
   investing   205, 208
loss leaders   157–8
loyalty programmes   74, 155, 166
Lululemon   153

257

INDEX

M
Manufacturer's Suggested Retail Price (MSRP)   153, 161, 166
marketing, awareness of   140
Marks & Spencer
  bonds   221
  shares   206
Mars bar analogy   63–4
MAT SPENDING PERSONALITY INDICATOR *see* MSPI
MBTI (Myers-Briggs Type Indicator)   21
medium-term saving and investing   205, 208
memberships   148
mental health problems and money   xiv–xv
merchant loyalty schemes   168–9
meta-habits   135, 137, 138
Microsoft Office   74
mindfulness   12
mindful spending, definition   11–15
mindset   197–9
money and life   38–9
Money Charity, The   82–3
money maestro   199
money off on future purchases   155
Money Savings Expert   89, 159
mood-based spending   37–8
mortgage   81, 82, 92
  affordability assessment   93
  downpayment   93, 94
  paying off   220

mortgage broker   219
mortgage house   93
mortgage industry teaser rates   159
MSPI   20–1
  CAT (Clueless/Accepting/Thoughtful) = Pleaser   28, 140, 142
  CDR (Clueless/Defiant/Reckless) = Ostrich   28, 140
  CDT (Clueless/Defiant/Thoughtful) = Hoarder   28, 140, 142
  IDR (Informed/Defiant/Reckless) = Dopamine Addict   29, 140
  impulsiveness   24, 27, 35–7, 130
  receptiveness   24, 26
  spending personalities   24–5
  survey   25–31
  types   140, 142
  understanding   24, 26, 130
MSRP (Manufacturer's Suggested Retail Price)   153, 161, 166
multiple accounts   122
Myers-Briggs Type Indicator (MBTI)   21

N
National Debtline   101
NatWest Premier Select current account   67
necessary expenses   120, 121
Nestlé   158
Netflix   73, 120, 121
Nice Gal syndrome   57–8

Nice Guy syndrome 57
Nightmare 28
 acceptance 33–4, 130
 authority 34–5
 change 36–7
 changing to Zen 33–7
 impulsiveness 35–7
Nike 103, 153
 gift card 164
non-automated required
  expenses 121
notes 221

O

Ocado delivery 74
Office of National Statistics
  (ONS) 106–9
operation at a Loss 157–8
Ostrich 28
out-of-the-money call options
  86
overcharging, company 57
overdraft facility 80, 82, 93
owed money, asking for 56, 57
own label products 175

P

packaging 147
parent groups at schools 49
Pareto Principle 62
PayPal 163
pension pot, average 15
pensions 205, 213–18

Perfect Spending Robot
  algorithm 12–14
personal bankruptcy
  90, 100–1
personal debt, UK 82–8
personal pensions 216
Pets At Home loyalty plan 166
phases of spending 133–8
 phase 1: no spend intention
  134–5
 phase 2: intent to spend 135–7
 phase 3: point of spend 137–8
 phase 4: after-spend reflection 138
physical cash 9–11
 imagining 145–6
Plato 127
Play Money 241–2
Pleaser 28
pocket money cards 243
Porsche 153
present audit 115–18
 surplus or deficit using monthly
  summary data 116–18
 timeframe for calculations
  115–16
price earnings ratio 226
Prime 73
progress, checking 190–1
property 205, 207, 218

Q

quality, cost and 53
Quidco 163

INDEX

R
rainy-day fund   110, 186–7
Rakuten   163
receipts   147
Reckless   32
relative value   146
repetition   191
Research in Motion   86
retailer discounts   165–6
Retail Inefficient Market Hypothesis   153
Retail Price Index (RPI)   167
retail therapy   184
retirement, planning for   189–90
reviewing spending   146
Roosevelt, Theodore   103
Rooster   243
RPI (Retail Price Index)   167
Rule of Zero   70, 71

S
Sainsbury's   157
  Nectar   166
sales   177
sales methods   153–5
Samsung   153, 154
S&P 500 index fund   207
Santander Everyday current account   67
saving plans by age   242–6
  baby to early primary years (age 0–6)   243

higher education and young adulthood (age 18+)   245–6
  junior stocks and shares ISA   243, 244
  older primary years (age 6–11)   244
  secondary school (age 11–17)   245
savings accounts   67–8
  children's   243
savings, average   15
savings companies   43–4
saying no   50
Schwed, Fred, Jr.: *Where Are the Customers' Yachts?* 208
seasonal activity   110
Self-Invested Personal Pension Plan (SIPP)   216, 227
seller ratings   177
selling   148
Seneca   179
shares   205–7
shopper, types of   159–61
shopping around   175–7
shopping subscriptions   74
shops and merchants   44
short-term saving and investing   205, 208
shyness   55–7
signing on bonuses   158–9
single account for day-to-day spending   226
SIPP pension   216, 227
Skipton   67

Index

smart meter 148
Smith, Will 41
smug, being 186
Snap 73
socialisation 192–3
social media 51–2, 240–1
 fraudulent sellers 177
 subscriptions 73
social pressure
 being a yes-person 47
 overcoming shyness 47
 pressure to participate 47–50
 social status 47
social spending 191–2
social status 51–5
software, by subscription 74
spending behaviours 21–3
 bad 23
 changing, example 31–3
 good 22–23
spending history 109–14
spending opportunities 8–11
spending personalities 24–5, 143
spending rules xvii–xviii
spending under duress 109
spending *vs* savings 5–8
Sports Direct 74
Spotify 73, 121
spread betting 223
Stakeholder pension 216
Stanford Marshmallow
 Experiment 236
state pension 216, 217

Stocks and Shares ISA 215, 227
straw-spend 70, 71
streaming services 148
student loans 81
subscriptions 73–5
Sunday Scaries 182
sunny-day fund 187–9
supermarkets 174–5
Switched-on Shoppers (SOS) 160

T
tax 213–18
teaser rates 158–9
Telegram 73
Tesco 157, 163
Tesco Clubcard 166, 174
Tesla 154–5
THOIL 194–5
Topcashback 162, 163
trading 204
Twain, Mark 41, 201

U
Uber Eats 76
UK
 debt in 81–2
 household spend pie 107
 personal debt in 82–8
 tax code 213
Ulster Bank 68
understanding 24, 26, 130
Universal Card Point Schemes
  (UCPS) 162, 165

unsecured loan 95
utilities 44–5, 148

V
vices 75–6
vouchers 155

W
waste 148
Wilde, Oscar 19

Wilson, Earl 79
wine 225–6
workplace pension 216, 227
Wrangler 73

Y
yes-person 57–8

Z
Zen 29, 31–3